U-Turns

Reversing the Consequences in Your Life

TONY EVANS

LifeWay Press®
Nashville, Tennessee

D1288494

EDITORIAL TEAM

Heather Hair
Writer

Reid Patton
Content Editor

Susan Hill
Production Editor

Jon Rodda
Art Director

Joel Polk
Editorial Team Lead

Brian Daniel
Publisher & *Manager, Adult Discipleship*

Brandon Hiltibidal
Director, LifeWay Adult Publishing

Published by LifeWay Press® • © 2020 Tony Evans

ISBN: 978-1-5359-0604-3
Item number: 005803941

Dewey decimal classification: 248.84
Subject heading: CHRISTIAN LIFE / DISCIPLESHIP / GOD--WILL

My deepest thanks go to Mrs. Heather Hair for her skills and insights in collaboration on this manuscript.

Unless indicated otherwise, Scripture quotations are taken from the New American Standard Bible®, Copyright © 1960, 1962, 1963, 1968, 1971, 1972, 1973, 1975, 1977, 1995 by The Lockman Foundation. Used by permission. (www.lockman.org) Scripture quotations marked NKJV are taken from the New King James Version®. Copyright © 1982 by Thomas Nelson. Used by permission. All rights reserved.

To order additional copies of this resource, write to LifeWay Resources Customer Service; One LifeWay Plaza; Nashville, TN 37234; fax 615-251-5933; call toll free 800-458-2772; order online at LifeWay.com; email orderentry@lifeway.com.

Printed in the United States of America

Groups Ministry Publishing • LifeWay Resources • One LifeWay Plaza • Nashville, TN 37234

Contents

About the Author

Dr. Tony Evans is the founder and senior pastor of Oak Cliff Bible Fellowship in Dallas, founder and president of The Urban Alternative, former chaplain of the NBA's Dallas Mavericks, and author of over 100 books, booklets, and Bible studies. The first African American to earn a doctorate of theology from Dallas Theological Seminary, he has been named one of the twelve most effective preachers in the English-speaking world by Baylor University. Dr. Evans holds the honor of writing and publishing the first full-Bible commentary and study Bible by an African American.

His radio broadcast, The Alternative with Dr. Tony Evans, can be heard on more than 1,400 US outlets daily and in more than 130 countries.

Dr. Evans launched the Tony Evans Training Center in 2017, an online learning platform providing quality seminary-style courses for a fraction of the cost to any person in any place. The goal is to increase Bible literacy not only in lay people but also in those Christian leaders who cannot afford nor find the time for formal ongoing education.

Dr. Tony Evans was married to his late wife, Lois, for nearly fifty years. They are the proud parents of four, grandparents of thirteen and great-grandparents of three.

For more information, visit TonyEvans.org.

How to Get the Most from this Study

This Bible study book includes six weeks of content for group and personal study.

Group Sessions

Regardless of what day of the week your group meets, each week of content begins with the group session. Each group session uses the following format to facilitate meaningful interaction among group members, with God's Word, and with the teaching of Dr. Evans.

START. This page includes questions to get the conversation started and to introduce the video teaching.

WATCH. This page includes key points from Dr. Evans's teaching, along with blanks for taking notes as participants watch the video.

DISCUSS. This page includes questions and statements that guide the group to respond to Dr. Evans's video teaching and to relevant Bible passages.

Personal Study

Each week provides three days of Bible study and learning activities for individual engagement between group sessions: "Hit the Streets" and two Bible studies.

SECURING YOUR U-TURN. This first personal exercise is meant to help you help you recognize the U-Turn you need to make and set your course for the week.

HIT THE STREETS. This section highlights practical steps for taking the week's teaching and putting it into practice.

BIBLE STUDIES. These personal studies revisit stories, Scriptures, and themes introduced in the videos in order to understand and apply them on a personal level.

D-Group Guides

In addition to the group sessions and personal studies, D-Group guides are provided at the back of this Bible-study book. These guides correspond to the six weeks of study and are designed to be used in a smaller group of three or four individuals for deeper discussion and accountability. Each guide provides helpful thoughts on the week's content and suggests a few questions for discussion by and accountability among the group.

TIPS FOR LEADING A SMALL GROUP

Follow these guidelines to prepare for each group session.

Prayerfully Prepare

REVIEW. Review the weekly material and group questions ahead of time.

PRAY. Be intentional about praying for each person in the group.

Ask the Holy Spirit to work through you and the group discussion as you point to Jesus each week through God's Word.

Minimize Distractions

Create a comfortable environment. If group members are uncomfortable, they'll be distracted and therefore not engaged in the group experience. Plan ahead by considering these details:

Seating   **Temperature**   **Lighting**

Food & Drink   **Surrounding Noise**

General Cleanliness

At best, thoughtfulness and hospitality show guests and group members they're welcome and valued in whatever environment you choose to gather. At worst, people may never notice your effort, but they're also not distracted. Do everything in your ability to help people focus on what's most important: connecting with God, with the Bible, and with one another.

Include Others

Your goal is to foster a community in which people are welcome just as they are but encouraged to grow spiritually. Always be aware of opportunities to include any people who visit the group and to invite new people to join your group.

An inexpensive way to make first-time guests feel welcome or to invite someone to get involved is to give them their own copies of this Bible-study book.

Encourage Discussion

A good small-group experience has the following characteristics.

EVERYONE PARTICIPATES. Encourage everyone to ask questions, share responses, or read aloud.

NO ONE DOMINATES—NOT EVEN THE LEADER. Be sure that your time speaking as a leader takes up less than half of your time together as a group. Politely guide discussion if anyone dominates.

NOBODY IS RUSHED THROUGH QUESTIONS. Don't feel that a moment of silence is a bad thing. People often need time to think about their responses to questions they've just heard or to gain courage to share what God is stirring in their hearts.

INPUT IS AFFIRMED AND FOLLOWED UP. Make sure you point out something true or helpful in a response. Don't just move on. Build community with follow-up questions, asking how other people have experienced similar things or how a truth has shaped their understanding of God and the Scripture you're studying. People are less likely to speak up if they fear that you don't actually want to hear their answers or that you're looking for only a certain answer.

GOD AND HIS WORD ARE CENTRAL. Opinions and experiences can be helpful, but God has given us the truth. Trust God's Word to be the authority and God's Spirit to work in people's lives. You can't change anyone, but God can. Continually point people to the Word and to active steps of faith.

Keep Connecting

Think of ways to connect with group members during the week.

Participation during the group session is always improved when members spend time connecting with one another outside the group sessions. The more people are comfortable with and involved in one another's lives, the more they'll look forward to being together. When people move beyond being friendly to truly being friends who form a community, they come to each session eager to engage instead of merely attending.

Encourage group members with thoughts, commitments, or questions from the session by connecting through these communication channels:

Emails   **Texts**   **Social Media**

When possible, build deeper friendships by planning or spontaneously inviting group members to join you outside your regularly scheduled group time for activities like these:

Meals   **Fun Activities**

Projects Around Your Home, Church, Or Community

Week 1

FREE TO CHOOSE YOUR DIRECTION

Start

Welcome to Group Session 1 of the U-Turns Bible Study.

What is the purpose of a u-turn while driving?

How can the concept of a u-turn apply to someone's choices?

As followers of Christ, we need u-turns in our lives to recover from wrong choices we've made in the past. Typically, wrong choices are rooted in sin. It could be our sin or someone else's sin against us, but blame is not my point. Sin, and its consequences, has a way of misguiding and misleading down the wrong path where we become stuck and wander aimlessly lost in the flashing lights, loud music, and chattering crowds.

Making a right turn here or a left turn there ultimately keeps you on the strip of sin. We need to do more than make a turn at the light. We need to do an about-face, otherwise known as a u-turn. Some people call this a complete 180. We need to choose to reverse our direction in order to exit the environment of sin, and its consequences, altogether, in order to pursue the pathway of peace and productivity God has chosen for us.

Invite someone to pray, then watch the video teaching.

Watch

Use these statements to follow along as you watch video session 1.

U-Turn: When God intervenes to enable you to see and experience life differently.

If you want to make a u-turn in your life, you're going to have to make a choice.

Death is separation from God.

Covenant: A divinely ordained relational agreement.

Video sessions available at lifeway.com/UTurns or with a subscription to smallgroup.com

Discuss

Use the following questions to discuss the video teaching.

Read Deuteronomy 30:15-20 together to answer the following questions.

God has given us a choice. Each of us has been given the ability to choose life or death, in everything we think, do, or say. Each moment is an opportunity to move forward into favor or backward into consequences and adversity. God doesn't make these choices for us. We have been blessed with free will to choose the course of our lives. The life we live today exists as the compounded result of myriad choices we've freely made along the way.

> **List some emotional obstacles which keep us from pursuing a path of life and prosperity (An example might be shame or regret). How do these obstacles keep us stuck in a cycle of wrong choices?**

> **What are the benefits of choosing what the Scriptures call the path of life rather than the path of death?**

Choices matter. They matter in life. They matter at work. They matter in sports. For example, in a football game, the players don't get to play on the sidelines or in the stands. These boundaries have been established by the NFL as sovereign marks indicating whether or not a player would be in or out of bounds. For better or worse, football teams get to choose the plays they run. But they don't get to choose the boundaries and rules within which those plays are to be run.

God has given each of us free will to make choices. But our choices produce results. Just as a football team's play would be blown dead by the whistle once the players stepped "out of bounds," our choices produce deadly results when we veer outside of God's sovereign guidelines. Now, those deathly results may not show up literally in something or someone dying. But they do show up regardless, whether it's a death in a relationship, dream, forward movement, or God's favor.

> **How have you seen this principle play out in your own life? What has happened when you stepped "out of bounds?"**

In the video Dr. Evans said, "When God created man, He created him with a will and the capacity to choose. God will not make the choice for you. What God will do is tell you the options on the table—you control the choice. But what you don't control are the consequences."

> **Why is it important to understand that choices have consequences that we cannot control? How would your decision-making process change if you were more aware of this truth?**
>
> **Share an example of when you experienced unexpected consequences of a bad choice.**
>
> **What would you say keeps believers from choosing to obey God on an ongoing basis?**

Dr. Evans described life as the ability to have God at work in you. Since God is life and Jesus came that we might have life and have it more abundantly (John 10:10), choosing to obey God naturally brings life and favor. God has established a process of choosing life through a covenantal agreement. This divinely ordained relational agreement gives you and I the freedom to make choices which will usher in God's presence, power, and provision in our lives as we follow the path of life outlined in the Scriptures. When we step off the path, God has a u-turn waiting for us.

> **What will you do this week to remember the path of life God has placed before you?**

Close in prayer.

PRAYER

Lord, open our hearts and minds during this series on u-turns so that we may fully grasp the importance of our momentary, ongoing choices and how they affect not only us, but those around us. Help us to learn from each other, share openly from the heart, and stay committed to the study and application of Your Word throughout our time together. In Jesus' name, amen.

Securing Your U-Turn

Use the following u-turn diagram to help you process the specific u-turn you need to make based on this week's teaching. Use the questions and statements on the next page to guide you through this exercise.

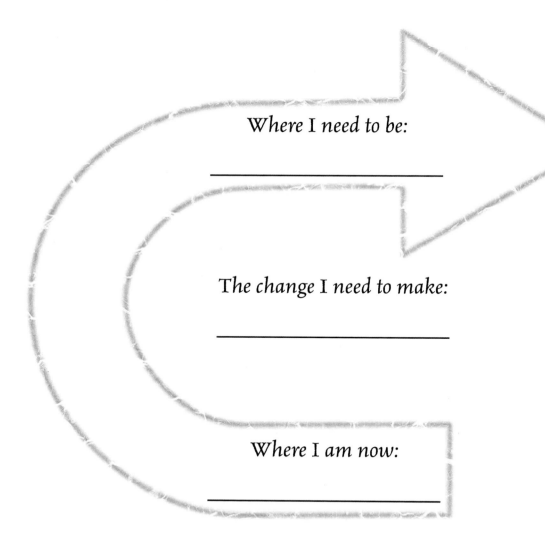

Where I need to be:

_____

The change I need to make:

_____

Where I am now:

_____

QUESTIONS TO CONSIDER

*Use these questions and statements to help you
fill out the diagram on the previous page.*

You are free to choose your direction. Consider where you are choosing the way of death and consequences. How might you choose life and blessing instead?

What are you hoping to gain out of this study?

What are some practical steps you can take toward life and blessing? How might you depend on the Spirit as you make God-honoring choices?

Hit the Streets
TRUST, LEAN, LOOK

The past three years have been the most challenging I've ever faced. Our family has experienced a disheartening amount of loss. I lost my brother, sister, brother-in-law, niece, father, and my precious wife all within a span of roughly two years. I know what it is like not to have the energy to walk out the door in the morning. But I also have come to know firsthand the power of peace.

When the walls of loss and uncertainty caved in around me, I discovered what it meant to say the name of Jesus and be filled with His peace. It's that peace and presence that got me through the days I could not get through in my own strength.

But peace only comes through choosing to align your heart, mind, and actions under the rule of God in obedience to Him. Peace grows out of the choices we make based on faith. It is nurtured and cultivated in a spirit of total dependence upon God and required surrender to His will. God gives us three principles in Proverbs 3:5-6 that will help us live in the favor of His peace.

Trust in the LORD with all your heart
And do not lean on your own understanding.
In all your ways acknowledge Him,
And He will make your paths straight.
PROVERBS 3:5-6

1. TRUST IN THE LORD WITH ALL YOUR HEART.

What would happen if you only trusted in the chair or couch you are sitting on, or will sit on later, with a half heart? What if you really didn't think it would hold you up? How would that change your behavior? Would you sit down gently and hold onto something else, in case it were to give way, and you were to fall? Or would you only sit for a short period of time? If you knew the chair or couch might collapse beneath you at any moment, you wouldn't flop down on it with all of your weight. Nor would you sprawl out and read a book or take a nap. Trust affects our choices. God wants you to trust Him with your whole heart so that your choices are influenced by that trust.

2. LEAN NOT ON YOUR OWN UNDERSTANDING.

I don't cook, but I have boiled an egg before. Once. I did it only once because I forgot about what I was doing, and walked away. The pan boiled dry and nearly caught on fire after being left on for so long. But anyone who cooks, or even just boils eggs, knows that in order for a meal, dessert, or snack to turn out—the cook needs to follow the instructions. Leaning on your own understanding, especially if you have limited understanding about ingredients like I do, can be disastrous at worst and tasteless at best. God made this world. He knows how it works. He knows what each of us must do in order to experience the abundant life. To make choices based on our own finite understanding while neglecting the instructions of the Master Chef is disastrous at worst and empty at best.

3. IN ALL YOUR WAYS ACKNOWLEDGE HIM.

To acknowledge God in all you do doesn't mean to reference Him or give Him a holy "shout-out." To acknowledge Him means to look to Him, to set your eyes on Christ and His way in order to know which way you are to move forward. It's all about where you choose to focus. Are you making your choices based on an eternal, kingdom perspective or on a limited, worldly perspective? Where you look determines where you'll wind up.

When you make the choice to trust in the Lord with all of your heart, to let go of your own way of understanding things and to look to God in everything you do, He will make your path straight. He will set you on the right road, headed in the right direction. He will give you peace.

How are you trusting God, right now, in this very moment for all you need?

BIBLE STUDY 1

THE HEART OF THE MATTER

Obedience involves aligning your thoughts, choices, and words with God's will. When you are in alignment, things generally work well. When you are not in alignment, you can expect to face the consequences of wrong choices. Remember, you are free to choose. You just don't get to choose the consequences that come attached to your choices. That's God's part in this equation called life.

One day I had gotten in my car to drive to the church when I pushed the garage door opener only to discover that nothing happened. Needing to get to a meeting, I decided to call the repairman. The first thing he asked me to do was walk over to the garage door and check to see if the sensors at the bottom were facing each other, or if one had gotten knocked to face another direction. This is because when the sensors fail to align with each other, the signal doesn't connect and the garage door won't raise. As soon as I turned the one sensor toward the other, my garage door opener worked just fine. I was free to leave—all because of this powerful thing called alignment.

Review Deuteronomy 30:17-18 and answer the following questions.

But if your heart turns away and you will not obey, but are drawn away and worship other gods and serve them, I declare to you today that you shall surely perish. You will not prolong your days in the land where you are crossing the Jordan to enter and possess it.
DEUTERONOMY 30:17-18

What does it mean to turn your heart away from God?

What does that look like in your own life?

**Contemporary culture doesn't always label idols as "other gods."
What are some idols that believers worship today?**

**When has making a wrong choice cut something short in your life—
a relationship, pursuit, career opportunity, or any number of things?**

What did you learn from that situation?

You serve what you obey. You worship what you align yourself with. Whoever, or whatever influences the final decision in your life, is an idol. If the ultimate determining factor in your life is not the true, living God and His Word, you are serving and obeying an idol.

What are some ways Satan subtly seeks to infiltrate disciple's lives and draw our worship away from God to something else?

How can becoming more aware of Satan's tricks to sway your worship from God help you steer clear of his schemes?

Matthew 6:24 describes the allegiance of our worship this way,

> No one can serve two masters; for either he will hate the
> one and love the other, or he will be devoted to one and
> despise the other. You cannot serve God and wealth."
> MATTHEW 6:24

For personal application, you can substitute wealth in there for whatever it is that comes before God's rule in your life and draws you from an intimate relationship with Him.

Here are a few more examples. The rest are blank for you to fill in with ones you may struggle with, or witness other people struggling with in our society:

I cannot serve God and **popular opinion.**

I cannot serve God and **people-pleasing.**

I cannot serve God and **dishonesty.**

I cannot serve God and **bitterness.**

I cannot serve God and **pride.**

I cannot serve God and _____.

I cannot serve God and _____.

I cannot serve God and _____.

I cannot serve God and _____.

I cannot serve God and _____.

I cannot serve God and _____.

You have to choose one or the other as the ultimate influencer over your decisions. You get to choose. Yet with those choices come consequences: Favor or futility. Essentially, you get to choose if you experience blessings or negative consequences in your life. You choose by what you do.

When you think about it, that's a really good thing. God has given you the option to choose whether you want favor or futility. It's up to you. You are free to choose. Following God's way might make parts of your life more challenging. Jesus, Daniel, Paul, and Moses, all experienced hardship following God, yet the favor of God remained with them because they obeyed Him in all things.

How do we differentiate hardships from good choices and consequences from negative choices?

Why is it critical to remain confident in God's compassionate love when we are going through the negative consequences of our wrong choices?

What happens to our view of God if we forget that our own wrong choices dictate our consequences?

God longs to bless you. His love for you is beyond anything you could ever fathom. But, because He loves you so much, He won't force His love on you. You get to choose how much of His loving presence, power, and favor you experience in your life. Just like in any relationship, it takes communication, honor, and love to nurture that connection. In Las Vegas, as we filmed this Bible study, I saw a lot of slot machines. But because we filmed this study right at the start of the national shutdown due to the COVID-19 pandemic, these slot machines were empty. The casinos were empty. In fact, we got notice while we were there filming that our hotel was closing down, and we had to get out of town right away.

The empty slot machines reminded me of how so many believers view God. To many people, He's a cosmic blessing-machine there to entertain us and occasionally drop some benefits in our hands. We pull His lever through prayer. But that's not how God works. God is not a machine. He's a relational being who loves you fully. Prayer is not a manipulative tool to get what you want. It's communication with God Himself.

Pray about your relationship with God and the choices you've made in the past that created relational separation between you and Him. Ask His Spirit to reveal where you have gone in the wrong direction. While you thank God for the gift of free will, ask Him to renew a healthy reverence for what that truly means.

BIBLE STUDY 2

COVENANTAL CONNECTION

When a man and wife get married, they become bound covenantally. A legal action has occurred. A wedding is more than a get-together or event. The covenant indicates that by law, the two are now related as husband and wife.

Consider what would happen to marriages, homes, and families if marriage wasn't a covenant. Consider if there was no legal binding at all, and it was a decision that could be changed in a moment's time based on emotion, choice, or preferences. How would that affect:

- Property ownership shared by spouses
- Raising children
- Intimacy in the marriage
- Financial responsibilities
- Fidelity to your spouse

All of those things, and more, would be turned upside-down in a heartbeat if marriage were simply a decision that can change on a whim. Certain roles and responsibilities apply to sharing life together, and when they're not taken seriously, chaos quickly ensues. Scripture often uses marriage as metaphor for God's relationship to His people. Like a marriage, God's relationship to His people is covenantal. Consider the following examples from Deuteronomy.

Read the following verses from Deuteronomy 29, and describe the different aspects of the covenant that show up in each. The first one has been filled in for you.

These are the words of the covenant which the LORD commanded Moses to make with the sons of Israel in the land of Moab, besides the covenant which He had made with them at Horeb.
DEUTERONOMY 29:1

Aspects of the covenant: ___God initiated the covenant __

So keep the words of this covenant to do them,
that you may prosper in all that you do.
DEUTERONOMY 29:9

Aspects of the covenant: _____

That you may enter into the covenant with the LORD your God, and
into His oath which the LORD your God is making with you today.
DEUTERONOMY 29:12

Aspects of the covenant: _____

Now not with you alone am I making this covenant and this oath,
but both with those who stand here with us today in the presence of
the LORD our God and with those who are not with us here today.
DEUTERONOMY 29:14

Aspects of the covenant: _____

Then the LORD will single him out for adversity from
all the tribes of Israel, according to all the curses of the
covenant which are written in this book of the law.
DEUTERONOMY 29:21

Aspects of the covenant: _____

Then men will say, 'Because they forsook the covenant of
the LORD, the God of their fathers, which He made with
them when He brought them out of the land of Egypt.
DEUTERONOMY 29:25

Aspects of the covenant: _____

A covenant is a divinely ordained and authorized relational bond. It is an official arrangement through which God reveals Himself, not a casual discussion. Israel was God's covenanted people. They belonged to Him in a formally arranged way. That's why in Deuteronomy 30:19, the language Moses used resembles language you would hear in a court of law. He says, "I call heaven and earth to witness against you today."

In what ways does understanding the covenant between God and His people shed light on the cause and effect nature of obedience or disobedience to His rule?

I often compare a covenant to an umbrella. An umbrella doesn't stop the rain from coming down. But when you are underneath the covering of the umbrella, it stops the rain from reaching you. Divine covering is a benefit of a covenant. Just as you would never keep your umbrella closed in a rainstorm, neither should you make choices that you know would squelch the blessings of God's covenant in your life.

When have you experienced the blessings of God's covenantal covering during a difficult season?

What would you say about a kingdom follower who willingly chose disobedience to God's rule in spite of knowing the blessing that comes from obedience?

Why do we so often treat obedience as a chore rather than a gift from God meant to bring a downpour of blessing into our life?

Jesus came that we might enter into a new covenant with God based on grace and the law of love (Matt. 22:34-40). Abiding in Christ aligns you under His covenantal care. To abide means to "hang out" or to "loiter."

Read Hebrews 7:22.

Jesus has become the guarantee of a better covenant.
HEBREWS 7:22

In what way is the new covenant that Jesus came to usher into existence a better covenant than the one based on the Mosaic law we've been reading about in Deuteronomy?

Why is the covenant with Jesus the ultimate u-turn?

What must a person do to enter into this better covenant which Jesus guarantees?

In Jesus, our relationship with God is eternally secure. He is always and forever pleased with us in Christ. Nevertheless, following Christ means seeking to follow the commandments of God with all of our heart, soul, mind, and strength. While security in our relationship with God is not dependent upon our obedience, willing obedience to God brings joy and contentment in the lives of kingdom citizens.

Pray right now and ask Jesus to reveal to you the areas of your life which need to align under His rule. Ask Him to draw you close into an abiding relationship so that you can experience the full benefits of this greater covenant. Repent of past sins and seek God's forgiveness. This will set you on the path toward experiencing the u-turns you need in order to fully live out your purpose in God's kingdom agenda on earth.

Week 2

THE KEY TO YOUR REVERSAL

Start

Welcome to Group Session 2 of the U-Turns Bible Study.

What was one lesson you took away from last week's session?

Last week we introduced the concept of u-turns. This week we will learn about the key that empowers us to make a u-turn.

Have you ever gotten off-track in life? If you feel comfortable, share what happened.

Have you ever unintentionally driven down the wrong road, only to discover you've driven past your destination? You knew you needed to turn, but you got distracted on the road, so you missed the spot to turn.

Now you're not only going in the wrong direction, but you've also missed the spot to turn around. If you're like me, you'll start looking for other ways to turn around because you missed the natural place to turn, you start looking for u-turns you can make yourself.

Sometimes this happens in life when too many wrong decisions have placed us on the wrong path, and we don't see a way to turn around. The good news is that even though you may have missed the exit, God can show you how to do a u-turn even when it seems there's no place left to make one. God always has a way.

Invite someone to pray, then watch the video teaching.

Watch

Use these statements to follow along as you watch video session 2.

Repentance is the master key that God uses to break the
binding that has held you spiritually hostage.

Sin is anything that deviates from the divine standard God has prescribed.

The goal of repentance is to restore fellowship with the living and true God.

Repentance is an internal decision and determination to turn from sin.

1 John 1:7-9: Repentance starts with the recognition of sin.

2 Corinthians 7:10: God wants you to be remorseful over your sin.

James 4:1-10: God wants you to turn from your sin.

Video sessions available at lifeway.com/UTurns or with a subscription to smallgroup.com

Discuss

Use the following questions to discuss the video teaching.

Read the words of Ezekiel together.

Again, when a wicked man turns away from his wickedness which he has committed and practices justice and righteousness, he will save his life.
EZEKIEL 18:27

Ezekiel teaches that repentance includes both turning from wickedness and practicing righteousness. Repentance is the master key to unlocking the kind of blessing and life we studied last week in Deuteronomy 30.

> **How does our relationship with Jesus empower us to be the kind of person described in the verse above?**

> **What does it mean to practice "justice and righteousness" in light of the grace given to us by Jesus Christ?**

Dr. Evans tells us in the video, "The goal of repentance is to restore fellowship with the living and true God." He goes on to explain, "Biblical repentance is the internal decision and determination to turn from sin." While forgiveness is entirely based on the sinless sacrifice of Jesus Christ, repentance still involves a determination to turn from sin. The goal of repentance is the restoration of fellowship with God. Living in continual sin hinders our fellowship with God.

> **Read 1 John 1:9-10. How would continuing in sin hinder the restored fellowship with God given to us by Jesus?**

> **Think of a time when you have sought reconciliation in a relationship. How did seeking forgiveness help your relationship? How has habitual repentance strengthened your relationship with God?**

In the video, Dr. Evans explains the difference between godly sorrow and being sorry that you got caught. He says that godly sorrow means "you're sad that you hurt the heart of God." Second Corinthians 7:10 says, "For the sorrow that is according to the will of God produces a repentance without regret, leading to salvation, but the sorrow of the world produces death."

In your own words, describe the difference between godly sorrow and "the sorrow of the world."

When David repented of his sexual sin with Bathsheba and the murder of Bathsheba's husband, he said, "Against You, You only, I have sinned and done what is evil in Your sight" (Ps. 51:4). Recognition that sin hurts the heart of God is at the root of biblical repentance. It's not merely a way to try and get out of negative consequences brought on by wrong choices. If restoring one's relationship with God is the goal, choices that align under His will be the result.

Why is repenting simply because we feel sorry only half-hearted repentance?

How does this half-hearted repentance keep us from making the u-turn God wants us to make?

Half-hearted repentance produces half-hearted obedience. Our actions will reflect God's desire for our lives only when we repent out of sincere love for Him. The root of righteousness rests in a relationship with God; it's not based on law, fear, or manipulating behavior seeking to skirt the consequences of sin. God sees our hearts, and He longs to connect authentically with each of us based on our desire to know and honor Him.

Close the session with prayer.

PRAYER

Father, give me a pure heart. Restore a right spirit in me. Let our repentance not merely be a clever way of seeking to get out of any negative consequences that we face. Show us what it means to experience Your presence when we repent. Give us a glimpse of Your delight and Your joy when we come to You in godly sorrow over wrong choices and the sins we have committed against You. In Christ's name, amen.

Securing Your U-Turn

Use the following u-turn diagram to help you process the specific u-turn you need to make based on this week's teaching. Use the questions and statements on the next page to guide you through this exercise.

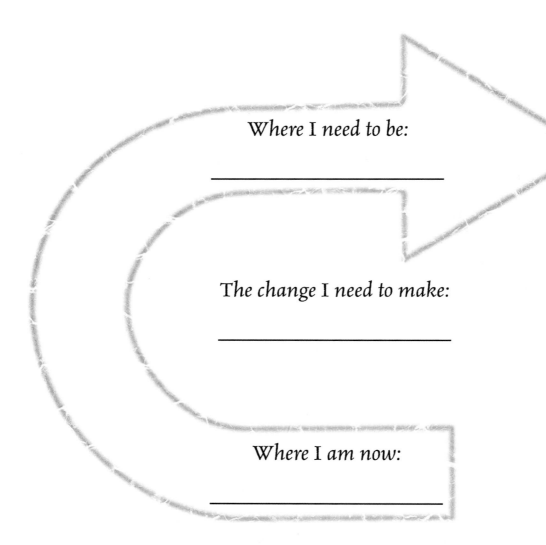

Where I need to be:

_____

The change I need to make:

_____

Where I am now:

_____

QUESTIONS TO CONSIDER

*Use these questions and statements to help you
fill out the diagram on the previous page.*

**Repentance is an ongoing process for a believer. Evaluate areas of your
life in need of repentance.**

**If you cannot think of an area for repentance, start by thinking about your
common struggles and hang-ups. What needs to happen to gain freedom
in those areas?**

**Spending time with God helps reveal our sins. What has your time with
God revealed to you lately?**

Hit the Streets
THE ROAD HOME IS ALWAYS THE FASTEST

Have you ever noticed when you are heading home from a long trip that the drive home seems so much faster than the drive you took going? The miles are the same. The time is the same. The distance is the same. But it feels quicker coming home. You know home. You can rest at home. Home represents comfort, familiarity, routine, predictability, and personal space, among many other things.

While sin may have gotten you off track and removed from God, know that the path home to His heart is a quick one. It doesn't take long at all, no matter how far you've gone in the wrong direction. God outlines this path to His heart in the Book of James, where he wrote:

> *Draw near to God and He will draw near to you. Cleanse your hands, you sinners; and purify your hearts, you double-minded.*
> JAMES 4:8

Let's take a brief look at each step of the process.

1. DRAW NEAR TO GOD.

God gives us great assurance in this passage that if we draw near to Him, He will draw near to us. That's one way to make up a lot of ground in a short time. As you move toward God, He is moving toward you. And, what's more, I imagine God moves faster than we do. Drawing near to God bridges the relational gap and restores your proximity to God in a flash.

2. CLEANSE YOUR HANDS.

With the onset of a global pandemic that came to light in 2020, we all learned well what it means to cleanse your hands. In fact, we were instructed to be sure and wash our hands a full 20 seconds each time, and make sure we got all the areas inside the thumbs and elsewhere. This is because unseen germs can lurk if a person simply does a quick wash of the hands. When God asks us to cleanse our hands of the sin that has ensnared us, He's asking us to cleanse them fully. He doesn't want a simple rinse and run. He wants us to fully rid ourselves of that which has plagued our hearts and separated us from His pure presence.

3. PURIFY YOUR HEARTS.

James makes a point of following up the call to purify our hearts with a statement on our minds. He calls out the "double-minded." Thus, to purify your heart is also to focus your mind. The two are related. As a man "thinks within himself, so he is," said the wise man in Proverbs 23:7. Purifying your heart also means directing your mind onto the truths of God and His Word. When your thoughts align with God's Word, your heart will follow.

When you make a choice to draw near to God, cleanse your hands and purify your heart while focusing your thoughts on the truth of God's Word, you will experience God's unique, intimate presence and power in your life. He can turn things around on a dime if you let Him.

Out of the three steps outlined in James 4:8, which do you need to pursue today? Why?

BIBLE STUDY 1
SIN'S SLIPPERY SLOPE

When a person has a master key to a facility, that means they can unlock any door. All doors are subject to this one key. Now, a person may have an individual key to their individual room, but someone with a master key can gain access into all the rooms. Simply stated, the master key for u-turning away from negative outcomes in your life brought on by sin involves developing a lifestyle of repentance. The possibility of the reversal of negative life circumstances rooted in wrong choices can only be found in repentance.

Sin is rarely a topic you hear much about today. It doesn't fit into the seeker-sensitive culture we are now in. Sure, we'll mention a mistake or lapse in judgment here or there. But say something about sin and people might get offended.

How would you define sin in your own words?

Review Romans 3:23. According to this passage, who has sinned?

Why is this important to realize?

What does it mean to "fall short of the glory of God?"

Sin is anything that deviates from God's divine standard. We are all sinners. Repentance is necessary because sin is real. Deny the existence of sin and you deny your own solution to the self-inflicting problems and consequences you face. Redefine sin and you have also removed your ability to turn from the negative outcomes of it.

.James wrote,

Therefore, to one who knows the right thing to
do and does not do it, to him it is sin.
JAMES 4:17

What are some examples of sin that would fit in the category of James 4:17:

*   _____
*   _____

*   _____
*   _____

Take a moment to participate in a visual illustration of sin's contaminating effects. I want you to get a glass and fill it with clean drinking water. Next, I want you to go outside and just grab a pinch of dirt. It doesn't need to be much. Similar to a pinch of salt, just grab a little. Once you've gotten your pinch of dirt, go ahead and drop it into the clean water you just poured. Now, stir it. Are you ready to take a drink? Or, would you give this to someone to drink? I hope you answered "no" to both of those questions.

Dirt contaminated the drink and made it undrinkable. Similarly, sin contaminates the soul whether it is a massive amount of sin or just a little white lie here or there. In the same way that a doctor or nurse wants the surgical room sterile because any bacteria, no matter how small, will contaminate the process, God's holiness demands that we address and repent of our sins however grievous or small they may be.

Unfortunately, many people are stuck traveling down the wrong road in life because they want God to leave their sin alone but get rid of their problems. Yet, sin is an affront to a holy God because it's a violation of His divine standard.

In what subtle ways does Satan seek to downplay the contaminating effects of what we often call "smaller" sins in our lives?

Which of your own sins are you downplaying as minor or excusable?

Whether the sins we commit are sins of commission (intentional sins) or sins of omission (unintentional sins), all sin leads to the same outcome: Separation from God's relational power and presence in our daily lives. We do not lose our salvation—but we do lose out on many of the benefits and blessings that intimate fellowship with God brings. The word "death" in Scripture doesn't always refer to a physical death. It might mean a death of a relationship, dream, path, or any number of things.

Read the following verses and respond below with how you've seen these consequences of sin play out in the world around you:

> *But from the tree of the knowledge of good and evil you shall not eat, for in the day that you eat from it you will surely die.*
> GENESIS 2:17

> *Behold, all souls are Mine; the soul of the father as well as the soul of the son is Mine. The soul who sins will die.*
> EZEKIEL 18:4

> *Then when lust has conceived, it gives birth to sin; and when sin is accomplished, it brings forth death.*
> JAMES 1:15

> *Return, O Israel, to the LORD your God, for you have stumbled because of your iniquity.*
> HOSEA 14:1

Have you ever tried to walk along the edge of a hill or cliff when the ground was wet and slippery? I have, and it isn't much fun. You must pay careful attention to every step you take. One wrong move and down the hill you go. The same can be said for sin. Sin has damaging effects on a person's life and it doesn't take much sinning before a person finds himself or herself facedown in the dirt.

Sin should never be taken lightly. Yet, because of God's overabundant grace, it often is. Paul put it this way:

> *What shall we say then? Are we to continue in sin so that grace may increase? May it never be! How shall we who died to sin still live in it? Or do you not know that all of us who have been baptized into Christ Jesus have been baptized into His death? Therefore we have been buried with Him through baptism into death, so that as Christ was raised from the dead through the glory of the Father, so we too might walk in newness of life.*
>
> ROMANS 6:1-4

What is Paul's reasoning for not continuing in sin?

In your own words, describe what it is meant by walking "in newness of life."

Violating God's rule in your life is not sin nor is it "my bad." It is sin, plain and simple. Whenever you violate, transgress, or ignore God's standard in your thoughts, actions, and words, you are sinning. You are going against God's nature. You are not walking in the newness of life which Christ's sacrifice has given to you. In order to walk in the victory which is your birthright as a child of the King, you must align your thoughts, words and actions under God's rule in your life.

Spend a few minutes praying to God and asking Him to help you take your sin seriously. Invite the Holy Spirit to search your heart, reveal your sin, and lead you in the path of forgiveness and freedom.

BIBLE STUDY 2
PUTTING IT BACK TOGETHER

Have you ever torn your socks or another piece of clothing? Maybe it was a piece of clothing that you liked, so, despite the damage, you didn't want to get rid of it. If you possess any skills with a needle and thread, or if you know someone who does, you probably did what many do when clothing tears—you stitched it back together.

Or, worse yet, maybe you took a nasty fall or experienced a wreck that required a doctor to stitch you up. Due to the careful stitching of the master, what once was torn apart ultimately formed back together over time. Repentance is God's way of sewing back together the rupture with Him.

Once that rupture is rejoined, the potential for reversing negative consequences exists. Yet none of this can occur without the personal, internal resolve and determination to 1) acknowledge our sin, 2) turn away from sin, and 3) move toward God. When you seek to repair your relationship with God through this internal resolve to deal with your sin, you have set the stage for healing to occur.

List the steps necessary for repentance?
1.

2.

3.

What happens if we exclude one of these steps?

How is repentance the catalyst for restoration when it comes to your relationship with God?

To see the necessity of all three steps in repentance, consider the biblical accounts of Judas (Matt. 27:3-5) and Peter (Luke 22:61-62; Acts 5:27-29)—both involved sorrow over wrong choices. Yet their sorrow led to two vastly different results.

Based on the Scriptures mentioned above, describe the differences in the outcomes of both of their sorrow:

Judas:

Peter:

Judas and Peter both acknowledged the sinfulness of their words and actions. Both men felt some level of sorrow. Yet only Peter repented. Repentance causes a change of heart demonstrated through a change in actions. Only Peter's repentance led to peace. Only Peter's response led to life. Only Peter's response created a u-turn, which brought about what Matthew 3:8 calls, "fruit in keeping with repentance."

What is an example of fruit that is in "keeping with repentance?"

In what ways does our contemporary culture often undermine the need for authentic repentance?

Repentance always includes a return to God. Zechariah 1:3 says, "Therefore say to them, 'Thus says the LORD of hosts, "Return to Me," declares the LORD of hosts, "that I may return to you," says the LORD of hosts."

What are some common hindrances that keep us from truly making our u-turn and "returning" to the Lord?

Repentance is deeper than worldly sorrow. It involves more than emotion. Repentance is an action you take to move in the opposite direction. God-honoring repentance is not merely a button you push; it's a process that transforms your heart.

Have you ever found yourself repenting robotically—like pushing a button, or saying a simple prayer almost by rote, or by memory, rather than truly repenting from your heart? What is lacking in this kind of repentance?

What steps or reminders could you put in place to help avoid falling into this temptation in the future?

If you really want to overcome Satan's dominance in your life and invite God's greater grace into the negative outcomes you face on a daily basis, it involves having sorrow over having grieved the heart of Almighty God. Repentance is like a sergeant saying:

ABOUT-FACE.

REVERSE.

SHIFT YOUR DIRECTION.

What would an "about-face" and reversal to shift your direction look like in practical steps for the following sins?

Lies:

Wasting time or conducting personal matters while on the clock:

Emotional or physical unfaithfulness in marriage:

Pride:

Gossip:

If you want to witness God intervene in your financial circumstances, or your emotional upheavals, or relational and spiritual mayhem, you must start by using the same master key called repentance. We all have to use this same key. It doesn't matter who we are, how big our platform is, how many social media followers we have, or how much we say (or sing) about loving God. This master key of repentance belongs to all of us. Our deliverance is in our repentance.

Read Acts 3:19-21. Based on this passage, what is the result of authentic repentance?

What is the source of that result?

In what other positive ways does "the presence of the Lord" impact our lives?

God longs to give you all of the blessings and benefits that accompany an intimate relationship with Him. Proximity to the One who rules over all will determine how much of the abundant life you are able to experience. But proximity to the pure, holy God can only come through the key called personal repentance.

> Pray for the courage to do an about-face and reversal from the sins that have dominated your life. Ask God to give you insight into any sins you have not repented of, but need to. Then bow before the holy God, rend your heart and repent. Ask Him to draw near to you as you draw near to Him. In His presence is peace, forgiveness, power, and love.

Week 3

REVERSING
IDOLATROUS
CONSEQUENCES

Start

Welcome to Group Session 3 of the U-Turns Bible Study

Thinking back to last week, why is repentance the master key?

This week we shift into working through specific u-turns each of us need, beginning with idols. We live in the era of the selfie. Everywhere you go, people are taking photos of themselves. If God were walking among us in human form at this time in history, though, He would not take a selfie. This is because one of the things God said to His people is that they should never make an image of the living God.

What comes to mind when you hear the word idol? What about idolatry?

The Israelites were strictly told not to carve, create, build, or fashion anything that would stand in resemblance of God. The only selfie God ever took in all of history was Jesus Christ. Jesus is God's selfie. Other than Jesus, He told humanity not to even attempt it because we would mess it up. At best, our attempts at making an image of God would be like a bad photograph you get from a photo booth machine. They are a cheap reflection of the real thing, and usually not something you show to very many people at all. They often distort reality. And in the spiritual realm, any distortion of who God truly is becomes idolatry, which is what we will be talking about this week.

Invite someone to pray, then watch the video teaching.

Watch

Use these statements to follow along as you watch video session 3.

God can't be second.

Idolatry is any noun—person, place, thing, or thought—that becomes your source.

God doesn't break us to hurt us; He breaks us to change us and
to bring us back into proper relationship with Him.

Don't let your independence keep you from bowing to the one true God.

Video sessions available at lifeway.com/UTurns or with a subscription to smallgroup.com

Discuss

Use the following questions to discuss the video teaching.

This week Dr. Evans taught on the story of Manasseh(2 Chronicles 33:1-20). Manasseh was living large when the reality of his crisis hit home. He was in control as the ruler and king of Israel. In fact, he became king at the tender age of 12. He knew little other than getting what he wanted when he wanted it. Scripture tells us that all of this power and popularity had gone to his head and, as a result, Manasseh "did evil in the sight of the LORD" (2 Chron. 36:12)

How does having cultural influence such as popularity and personal power lure us into dangerous sins like pride and self-sufficiency?

How can we keep these blessings from drawing us into unhealthy habits and sin?

Manasseh was raised in a faithful home. His father was Hezekiah, a righteous king. But, even so, he chose to do evil. He promoted and led a culture of evildoers and idolaters. Manasseh built high places where false gods could be praised and worshiped. He led his own family astray, sacrificing his own children to these idols. What's more, he led his whole nation astray. The entire nation wound up worshiping idols because their leader took them in that direction.

Because of that, judgment fell. God will not accept or allow competition to His rightful place in lives, families, and nations. Thus, God had to let Manasseh know that there is only one God, and Manasseh wasn't Him.

What things in your life tend to draw you away from God when you aren't keeping a close watch over your heart and habits?

In the video, Dr. Evans said that when someone is on the detour of idolatry, God "will invade our circumstances and He will let us know He is the only God and He is the only source by putting us in situations where our own resources can't get us out of." He described it as being taken from the palace to the pit when God strips a person or breaks him or her of personal superiority and prideful idolatry.

Why is God both kind and gracious to strip us of our idols?

How do loss and hardship have a way of revealing our idols?

God had to break Manasseh of his pride, so God humbled him. Thankfully, Manasseh was open to learning. Because in 2 Chronicles 33:13 we read, "When he prayed to Him, He was moved by his entreaty and heard his supplication, and brought him again to Jerusalem to his kingdom. Then Manasseh knew that the LORD was God." God had let things get really bad, so that they could ultimately get a lot better. Loss revealed his idol and empowered his u-turn.

What specific steps can you take this week to make a u-turn from pride or idolatry? Even if it is a small step, take that step.

Close the session with prayer.

PRAYER

Father, there are times when you allow difficulties and challenges to arise in order to help us to learn the importance of humility and dependence on You. Help us to learn these lessons without having to experience great pain. Give us the grace to learn well and quickly, and to apply what we've learned. We want to honor You above all—please teach us gently so that we can repent and return to You. In Jesus' name, amen.

Securing Your U-Turn

Use the following u-turn diagram to help you process the specific u-turn you need to make based on this week's teaching. Use the questions and statements on the next page to guide you through this exercise.

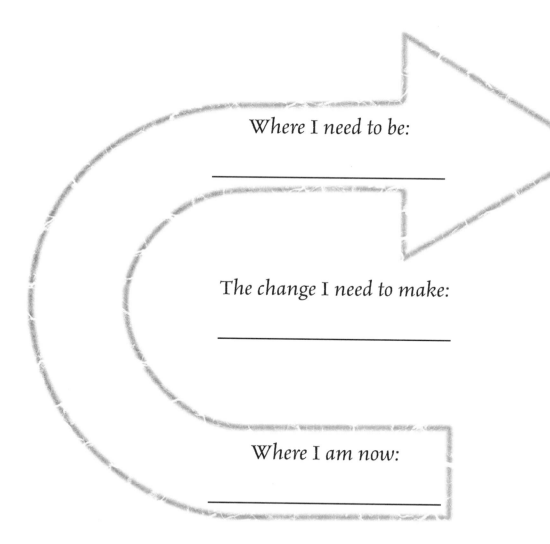

Where I need to be:

_____

The change I need to make:

_____

Where I am now:

_____

QUESTIONS TO CONSIDER
Use these questions and statements to help you
fill out the diagram on the previous page.

For most of us, idols are not statues made of wood and metal. Idols are the things that take our time and attention away from God. They are where our thoughts naturally go when we are at rest.

Spend a few moments in silence followed by a few moments in prayer asking God to reveal your idols.

Now that you see what your idols are, what steps do you need to take to let them go?

Who might help hold you accountable with your desire to have a u-turn from idolatry?

Hit the Streets
THREE THINGS TO DO IN THE PIT

Sometimes God allows difficulties in our lives by His own directive in order to produce the u-turn that will guide our hearts back to Him. The life story of Manasseh illustrates this reality well. We read about how the Lord dealt harshly with Manasseh's sin of idolatry in 2 Chronicles 33:11-13a. But we also read about how Manasseh responded to God's discipline and got back on the right path. Manasseh's life lesson gives us three key insights into how we can respond when faced with the consequences of sin in our lives. These insights are revealed to us in this passage:

> *The LORD spoke to Manasseh and his people, but they paid no attention. Therefore the LORD brought the commanders of the army of the king of Assyria against them, and they captured Manasseh with hooks, bound him with bronze chains and took him to Babylon. When he was in distress, he entreated the LORD his God and humbled himself greatly before the God of his fathers. When he prayed to Him, He was moved by his entreaty and heard his supplication.*
> 2 CHRONICLES 33:11-13A

1. HE ENTREATED THE LORD HIS GOD.

When Manasseh found himself in a bind, literally with hooks and bronze chains, he realized that even though he was the king of Israel, he wasn't the King over all. It took being in the pit in order to help him understand the rightful preeminence of God. When life turns sour due to our own sins, our first response ought to be like Manasseh's. The king entreated God—to "entreat" literally means to "beg." In the words of my favorite musical group, The Temptations, he "ain't too proud to beg." Manasseh learned the hard way that pride leads to destruction.

2. HE HUMBLED HIMSELF GREATLY.

The next part of the passage tells us that Manasseh humbled himself greatly before God. To humble yourself means to come to an awareness of who you are in light of who God is. It means releasing pride as you realize that pride is merely a tool of the devil to create division between you and the One who loves you most. Manasseh learned the hard way the principle found in Proverbs 16:18, "Pride goes before destruction, and a haughty spirit before stumbling." But the good news is that he did learn. No one is too far gone that they cannot humble themselves before God and entreat Him for His mercy.

3. HE PRAYED TO HIM.

Once Manasseh humbled himself to a proper position under the Almighty King, he proceeded to pray. He expressed his need for God's forgiveness and intervention to turn things around. We too, can go boldly to the throne of grace at any time we need due to the access we have gained through the sacrifice of Jesus Christ (Heb. 4:16). When God hears our prayer and sees the humility of our heart, He responds. He did so with Manasseh, and we can expect Him to do so with each one of us when we approach Him in humility and love.

Pride and idolatry often lead to very difficult lessons. Humility rarely comes without a cost, and the cost is often tied to our emotional or physical comforts, or both. But when we learn the lessons of humility and dependence on God, He can restore us to a place of dignity, hope, and healing that will benefit others and bring Him glory.

What practical steps do you need to take this week to protect your life from falling into the same kind of pit Manasseh fell into?

BIBLE STUDY 1

GO LOW

Abominations and idolatry are words that have fallen out of common usage. As a result, we tend to think these words don't apply to our lives today. After all, aren't abominations those things done in far-away temples in front of ten-story statues in a distant day and age? The Bible uses these words in specific ways, and to understand how God is calling us to live, we need to understand the meaning of these terms. It helps to put these biblical ideas in context; otherwise, we may flippantly dismiss them and assume we would never commit them ourselves.

Abominations include all of the sins of idolatry, which involve placing any thought, thing, or person ahead of God's rightful rule and place of honor in our hearts. What the Bible calls an "abomination," the culture often calls cool because abominations are also done today in our culture and in our own style, methods, and ways.

Read Exodus 20:4-5a and Colossians 3:5.

You shall not make for yourself an idol, or any likeness of what is in heaven above or on the earth beneath or in the water under the earth. You shall not worship them or serve them; for I, the LORD your God, am a jealous God …
EXODUS 20:4-5A

Therefore consider the members of your earthly body as dead to immorality, impurity, passion, evil desire, and greed, which amounts to idolatry.
COLOSSIANS 3:5

What are some common images we have in our contemporary culture which evoke our worship, awe, wonder, attention, or allegiance?

In what ways do we "serve" any of these contemporary idols?

Colossians 3:5 lists immorality, impurity, passion, evil desire, and greed as roots that contribute to idolatry.

What forms of idolatry can grow out of those various sins that may not have been listed in the answers to the first two questions?

Idols exist everywhere. They aren't just wood carvings. There are educational idols. Social idols. Relational idols. Entertainment idols. Sports idols. Gender idols. Cause idols. Economic idols. We advertise personalities and platforms today as if they are gods. People spend hours upon hours each day scrolling through pictures on Facebook, Instagram, Twitter, and the like following foolish people—crazy, indecent people who just so happen to look good or know how to edit a photo. Culturally, we give untold hours of our time to serve idols and distractions, and yet we can't find five minutes to spend with God or reading His Word.

To say that we are a nation of idol worshipers is an understatement. Yet the God of creation does not stand for competition. He has an exclusivity clause and a no-compete contract. Thus, whenever you bring in competition or idolatry against His rightful place in your life, you will be driving in the wrong direction. You will have made the Almighty God your enemy.

Where have you seen the kinds of idols listed above at work today? In your own life?

How does Satan utilize culturally acceptable idols to draw our hearts away from God?

What would you say are some of the most undetected "idols" in Christian culture today?

Ezekiel 14:6 reads,

> *" Therefore say to the house of Israel, 'Thus says the Lord*
> *GOD, "Repent and turn away from your idols and turn*
> *your faces away from all your abominations."*
> EZEKIEL 14:6

To turn your face away from something means to turn toward the opposite direction. It involves an about-face or a u-turn. It's exactly what we are talking about in our time together during this study.

When it comes to sin, each of us is given the opportunity to turn away from it ourselves (1 Cor. 10:13). But, as in the case of Manasseh, not everyone chooses to turn away. When that happens, God intervenes. He allows circumstances to come into our lives, which will humble us to the point of recognizing His lordship over all things.

When has God given you a u-turn away from your idols? What was that like?

At times, God has to drive us to our knees. This is exactly what He did with Manasseh. God stripped him of his independence. He broke him of his self-sufficiency. He had called for voluntary surrender, but when Manasseh refused to hear Him, God gave him a reason to look up. Sometimes humanity just needs a little help in humility.

According to Hebrews 12:6, why does God discipline us when we are in the midst of ongoing sin?

In football, the biggest players have to get the lowest in order to make the play. The larger you are, the lower you had better bend. Some of these players on the offensive or defensive line are over 300 lb. These men are huge. But in order for them to carry out their role to the best of their abilities, they have to crouch down low. This helps stabilize them before the play and also gives them greater access to their core strength.

Similarly, you and I will most fully live out our destiny in life when we humble ourselves and go low. God honors you when you humble yourself before Him. It is through humility that you find your path to purpose.

James 4:6 says, "But He gives a greater grace. Therefore it says, 'God is opposed to the proud, but gives grace to the humble.'"

On a scale of 1-10 (with 10 being the most):

How much is God opposed to the proud?
1   2   3   4   5   6   7   8   9   10

What makes it difficult to remember this truth in our daily lives?

How much does pride dominate your thoughts and actions?
1   2   3   4   5   6   7   8   9   10

Are you willing to ask God to release you of your attachment to pride, and create in you a humble heart?

Pray about your pride. Pray about any idols which are erected in your heart. Ask God to gently lead you toward a lifestyle of humility so that you will come to experience His grace in the fullest possible way. When you humble yourself before the Lord, He will lift you up (Jas. 4:10).

BIBLE STUDY 2
BROKEN TO BE BLESSED

Do you remember the Lone Ranger—the masked hero who battled outlaws in the wild west? The Lone Ranger saw a horse, but the horse was a wild stallion. The horse wouldn't let the hero ride him. The Lone Ranger would climb on, but the horse would buck him off.

Instead of giving up and walking away, the Lone Ranger would climb back on again. And, again, he'd get bucked off. This went on time and time again until eventually, the horse learned that the Lone Ranger wasn't about to stop. He was willing to climb on and get bucked off as many times as necessary to break the horse of its independence. This is because the Lone Ranger saw something in the wild stallion. He saw something special.

Guess what? God only breaks us because He sees something in us worth pursuing. God breaks us of our independence in order for us to align ourselves under His direction. As long as we are independent, we will simply wander through life alone. Yet when we yield to the mighty hand of God over our hearts, He gives us the ability to do and accomplish so much more.

For some of us, that breaking can come quickly. For others, it takes trial after trial after trial before we will humbly submit to God? Some of these trials include:

Loss

Health challenges

Relational conflicts, (fill in the blanks):

_____

_____

_____

Trials bring us a greater awareness of God's rightful place in our hearts. If we cooperate with the process, they can produce something wonderful in us, maturing us to the point of spiritual usefulness in the kingdom of God. But far too often, if we have gone a long time in the opposite direction from God's will for our lives, we may feel that we cannot return. Yet, God's Word reminds us that we are never too far from God's redemptive hand.

Read Isaiah 59:1-2.

> *Behold, the LORD'S hand is not so short that it cannot*
> *save; nor is His ear so dull that it cannot hear.*
> ISAIAH 59:1-2

What does this verse teach those of us who feel we are outside of God's reach?

God can meet you in the darkest places of your life and even in the furthest reaches of your disobedience and dishonor. Not only can He meet you, He can redeem you. You are never too far gone for God to restore you. You have not driven down the wrong road for too long that there is no way back. Humble your heart before the Lord, turn away from the idols that have ensnared you, and He will meet you where you are. He will lift you up.

Why is it important to remember that we are never too far from God to make a u-turn?

Who do you know that is far from God and in desperate need of a u-turn? How might you steer them in that direction?

U-Turns

Read the following verses and write in your own words God's response to our humility:

For though the LORD is exalted, Yet He regards the lowly, But the haughty He knows from afar.
PSALM 138:6

Though He scoffs at the scoffers, Yet He gives grace to the afflicted.
PROVERBS 3:34

A man's pride will bring him low, But a humble spirit will obtain honor.
PROVERBS 29:23

Whoever exalts himself shall be humbled; and whoever humbles himself shall be exalted.
MATTHEW 23:12

He has brought down rulers from their thrones, And has exalted those who were humble
LUKE 1:52

God gives grace to the humble and contrite in spirit. He lifts up those who bow low before Him. He restores the wayward soul. And He does all of this out of a heart of compassionate love. One attribute we don't always associate with God is His emotions. Sure, we may recognize His anger. But God also has a very caring heart. When Manasseh humbled himself, it moved God. He felt it. True repentance and humility move God's emotions. When He sees that you are not playing Him or seeking to manipulate Him, His mercy and grace abound.

According to Psalm 103:10-12, how does God treat the sins of His children?

God has seen what you have done. He knows how long you've done it and how deep it is. But He also wants to see how long you are going to let the devil hold you hostage out of fear. He wants to see how long you are going to allow Satan to control you, define you, and misdirect you.

God stands ready to forgive you and grant you a u-turn in life, but it is up to you to come to Him in humility and honesty. He's waiting. He's near. Wouldn't it be nice to have Him take you back to where you belong? If you know God through a relationship with Jesus, the Scriptures tell us your Father in heaven no longer remembers your sins and lawless deeds (Heb. 10:17). They are forgiven and driven as far away from you as the east is from the west. Turn back to Him. His arms are not crossed; they are open and ready to receive you.

> Pray right now to humble your heart before the Lord and seek His hand of grace and mercy in your life. He will hear your prayer and restore you to right fellowship with Him.

Week 4

REVERSING ADDICTION CONSEQUENCES

Start

Welcome to Group Session 4 of the U-Turns Bible Study.

Share one truth you learned about idolatry from the last session?.

Last week we looked at the most widespread stronghold, one we all fall victim to—idolatry. This week we are going to examine another—addiction.

Describe some addictions that don't fall within the obvious categories of drugs, alcohol, or pornography? (Example: approval addiction)

Have you ever tried to listen to an AM station at the same time as an FM station? Or, have you ever tried to watch one channel while also watching another (not using picture-in-picture)? Tuning into two things at once isn't possible because both broadcast on separate channels.

God and Satan are not on the same channel. God's way and the world's way of doing things are not the same. If you are flipping back and forth between God's viewpoint and the devil's viewpoint on addictions or how to break free from them, you'll remain stuck. Satan deceives us about our addictions by downplaying their severity. He wants you to believe it's only a hobby, or that you have a right to some entertainment. And while entertainment and hobbies are good, when the thing you are doing owns and dictates your time more than you do, it has become an addiction. It's only when you fully focus and commit to God's truth that you will discover His power to set you free.

Invite someone to pray, then watch the video teaching.

Watch

Use these statements to follow along as you watch video session 4.

Addiction is a spiritual stronghold of negative patterns of behavior for which you cannot be released so that you can move forward in spiritual victory.

Freedom is release from an illegitimate bondage holding you illegitimately hostage.

Truth is an absolute standard by which reality is measured.

God's statement on any subject is the truth.

Video sessions available at lifeway.com/UTurns or with a subscription to smallgroup.com

Discuss

Use the following questions to discuss the video teaching.

Read John 8:36 together.

So if the Son makes you free, you will be free indeed.
JOHN 8:36

Freedom—the word strikes at the core of who we are. With the onset of COVID-19 and the resulting nationwide lockdown, the restrictions on travel, and the extra precautions placed on our daily lives, we grew much more aware of our freedoms. Those of us who may have once taken our freedoms for granted got a fresh awareness of how valuable they are. Addiction robs us of our freedom.

A person can be free but not really free at all. A person can live in a nation of freedoms but still be bound by emotional, relational, or physical strongholds. Personal freedom sits at the root of addictions. You can't be both free and addicted at the same time. You will either be one or the other.

Fundamentally, addiction is a spiritual stronghold of negative patterns of behavior from which you cannot be released so that you can move forward in spiritual victory. We need Jesus to find the u-turns from our addictive behavior.

What are some common addictions we see in our context? How do these rob us of freedom?

How can a lack of personal freedoms due to our emotions, choices, and thoughts stifle personal growth, enjoyment, or achievements?

Freedom matters to all of us. Whether we are speaking of freedoms we experience as citizens of this country or the personal freedoms we experience within our own hearts, minds, and bodies—the extent to which we honor and enjoy freedom impacts the extent to which we can fully express our destinies in this life.

Dr. Evans defined freedom as, "release from illegitimate bondage holding you illegitimately hostage." How would you respond to this definition?

He went on to say that freedom is both your right and your responsibility.

In what ways are freedoms a responsibility? What happens to freedoms when they are not handled responsibly?

In the video Dr. Evans gave us three-step process to be set free from illegitimate bondage through strongholds and addictions. He said we must 1) know the truth, 2)abide in the truth, and then 3) allow Jesus to set us free.

Describe the importance of each step of this process in your own words. How would missing or skipping any one of these three critical components sabotage the steps to experiencing true freedom?

The approach to being set free was compared to that of scrubbing off food from dirty dishes versus allowing the dishes to soak and then letting the grime and food slide off. Dr. Evans explained that the former is the way most of us approach overcoming addictive behaviors and thoughts. But that the latter is the way that works.

Why do you think the process of abiding in Christ and knowing the truth of God's Word loosens the grip of addictive strongholds in a person's life more so than any other approach?

Close the session with prayer.

PRAYER

Father, release me from any and all illegitimate strongholds and bondage in my life. Whether it be wrong-thinking, behavior, words that I speak about myself or to others about others—whatever it is—I want to be free. Replace the lies with the truth of Your Word. Help me abide in Your Word and in Your presence so that I can know what it truly means to live free indeed. In Christ's name, amen.

Securing Your U-Turn

Use the following u-turn diagram to help you process the specific u-turn you need to make based on this week's teaching. Use the questions and statements on the next page to guide you through this exercise.

Where I need to be:

_____

The change I need to make:

_____

Where I am now:

_____

QUESTIONS TO CONSIDER
Use these questions and statements to help you
fill out the diagram on the previous page.

Dr. Evans defined addiction as a spiritual stronghold of negative patterns of behavior from which you cannot be released so that you can move forward in spiritual victory. What addictions are you suffering from?

Once you have identified your addictions, spend time praying for God to release you and bring you freedom. Write your prayer below.

How do all of us deal with addictions in one way or another? Why is it important to realize this is a problem we all deal with? How might you find support from another brother or sister in Christ here?

Hit the Streets
BE SET FREE

Have you ever gotten a kite stuck in a tree? Or what about a dog on a leash that gets wound up around something outside? Have you ever tried to open a kitchen drawer only to have something jam it stuck, and you have to figure out how to free it in order to open the drawer? Things get stuck in our lives. They just do. But when they do, rarely does the person just walk away and leave the kite, the dog, or the kitchen drawer shut. They wiggle it, tug it, unwind it, reach-in, and move it—do whatever it takes to get the thing set free. We would think it strange if someone just decided to walk away without even trying.

Unfortunately, when we find ourselves stuck in an addictive way of thinking or a stronghold of a negative behavior, far too many of us stay stuck. We feel trapped and see no way out so we don't even try, or we give up after trying something that doesn't work.

But God has given us a way out. We looked at in our video session discussion questions and it is so important, that we are going to review it here. We are set free through the three principles found in John 8:31-36:

> *So Jesus was saying to those Jews who had believed Him, "If you continue in My word, then you are truly disciples of Mine; and you will know the truth, and the truth will make you free."*
> JOHN 8:31-32

1. KNOW THE TRUTH.

Truth is not what you believe to be true. Truth is not what you feel to be true. Truth is an absolute standard by which reality is measured. Let me put it in everyday language: Truth is whatever God says about a subject. Whatever God says about a matter, regardless of how you think about it, feel about it, how you were raised about it, how much pressure is coming to you about it, is the truth. God is the one and only source of truth.

2. ABIDE IN THE TRUTH.

Yet, knowing the truth isn't all you need in order to be set free. You also need to abide in the truth. You can't just cognitively acknowledge it; you've got to hang out with the truth. Then truth begins to loosen the grip that Satan's lies had on you. How do you hang out with the truth? The same way you hang out with anyone. You wouldn't invite someone to come over and hang out at your place and then once they arrived, escort them out the door after two or three minutes. That would confuse them. It would also be rude. Yet that's how many of us approach God's Word and His presence. We spend a few minutes with God in the morning and call that abiding. That isn't abiding, and that flippant approach to God's Word can't set you free.

3. LET JESUS SET YOU FREE.

Once you know the truth and make time to abide in the truth with the presence of Jesus Christ, you can rest because Jesus will set you free. The truth of God's Word will peel away the vice grip of Satan's claws. In short, Jesus will do the work of breaking the bondage of your addictive behavior or thoughts.

Knowing the truth, abiding in the truth, and then trusting Jesus to set you free is the way to experience the abundant life promised you as a kingdom disciple (John 10:10). But it begins by making a commitment of your focus and time in such a way that you honor the power of God's Word by willingly concentrating on the truth of His Word.

To you, what does it mean to "abide in" or "remain in" the truth of God in an ongoing basis? Describe this in practical terms and activities.

BIBLE STUDY 1
THE STRUGGLE IS REAL

The biblical term for an addiction is "stronghold." The word stronghold refers to both the physical and spiritual nature of the addiction. An addiction is really a spiritual stronghold—an entrenched pattern of negative thoughts and actions that we believe to be unchangeable even though it is against the will of God. It's a sin that has become a slave-master over our thoughts, decisions, and actions.

Read Romans 7:14-15 then answer the following questions.

For we know that the Law is spiritual, but I am of flesh, sold into bondage to sin. For what I am doing, I do not understand; for I am not practicing what I would like to do, but I am doing the very thing I hate.
ROMANS 7:14-15

What does it mean to be "sold into bondage to sin?" What does that indicate about their life?

How do you relate to Paul's struggle? When have you done things you wished you hadn't?

How does this create further bondage to spiritual strongholds?

Paul summarized the way many people feel when they're bound by spiritual strongholds. These strongholds make us feel as if we are compelled to do the very things we didn't want to do. That can feel helpless like you no longer have the power to make your own decisions and choices.

Yet while many of us recognize the power of strongholds in our lives, most of us downplay the severity of those strongholds by excusing them as bad habits or mistakes.

But Paul doesn't call these strongholds bad habits. He names it for what it is: sin. It's not just a struggle. It's not just a challenge. It's sin. And in order for you to overcome this stronghold of sin in your life, you need to call it what it is. The addiction you seek freedom from is sin. Once we recognize sin for what it is, we can unlock our u-turn using the master key of repentance. We can answer our struggles the same way Paul did in Romans 7:25, "Thanks be to God through Jesus Christ our Lord!" Jesus is the one and only answer to our struggle with sin.

How should your faith in Jesus help free you from the addictions that plague your heart and mind? (refer back to John 8:31-36)?

Why must we treat the spiritual root of our addictions and not merely the physical and emotional fruit of our problem?

Far too many people simply seek to fix the physical and emotional aspects of an addiction without addressing the spiritual nature of it as well. This leads to failure and entrapment because all addictions are rooted in the spiritual. They derive their power from the same source, emanating from a space beyond the five senses of our routine reality. Spiritual addictions produce spiritual death.

Read James 1:14-15.

> *But each one is tempted when he is carried away and enticed by his own lust. Then when lust has conceived, it gives birth to sin; and when sin is accomplished, it brings forth death.*
> JAMES 1:14-15

What is the progression outlined for us in this passage?
1.

2.

3.

Why is it important to recognize a stronghold or addictive behavior as a sin, as compared to a bad habit or a mistake?

Once you realize the spiritual stronghold of addiction is sin that has you bound, you can repent and look to Christ for the next step. Though, when you do, He may ask you a surprising question. I say that because He did just that when people approached Him to be set free during biblical times. Jesus occasionally asked people whether they wanted to be made whole (John 5:5-6). If a person is stuck and wants to remain stuck, there's little anyone else can do to get them moving in the right direction. Freedom from addictive behavior starts with the recognition you are stuck and the desire to make a u-turn. You have to choose to get off the existing path and head in a different direction.

Why do you think Jesus asked the lame man if he wanted to be made well (John 5:5-6)?

Knowing how critical it is for the individual to want to be made well, what is the most effective and strategic thing to do for loved ones or friends struggling in addictive behavior?

Being bound by a spiritual stronghold is not like being locked in a prison without a key. Addiction is not an inevitable reality. You can be set free. But it starts by acknowledging it as a sin and then going to God with a heart that wants to be made well.

You have every right and opportunity to be completely set free from whatever strongholds entangle you. You are not the only person, nor are you the first person to struggle for freedom. Even the great apostle Paul struggled with something he had difficulty shaking, as we saw earlier. He was serious about overcoming it. But he still struggled between the pull of his flesh and the power of his spirit. The two simply couldn't get along.

What are some common struggles you face between your flesh and the spirit?

Why is it important to only focus on God and His view of these struggles, rather than on worldly approaches or sheer will-power to overcome them?

When Jesus raised Lazarus from the dead, we are told that Lazarus came up from his tomb tied up in his hands and feet. Just because he had been restored to life didn't mean that he was free. Lazarus was still bound. That's why Jesus instructed those around him to loosen what bound him. Life and freedom do not always come hand in hand. Many are alive who are not yet free. Pursuing Jesus and abiding in Him unleashes the Spirit's power to set us free.

Pray about the need you have to be set free from anything that is holding you hostage at this point. Ask God to help you see the sinful root of any addictive behavior or thoughts you struggle with, in order to start the process of repenting and turning from that which holds you back from fully living out your purpose for His kingdom.

BIBLE STUDY 2

THE WHOLE TRUTH AND NOTHING BUT THE TRUTH

When you are sick and you go to the doctor, the doctor is going to try to find the cause of your ailment. He or she needs to locate the cause so they can give you the right cure. Hopefully, your doctor doesn't just guess.

Not too long ago, I came down with a case of pneumonia. In fact, it was shortly after filming this Bible study. When I went to the doctor, they didn't just test for pneumonia. They tested for a lot of things because they wanted to rule out any other issues to get an accurate diagnosis. Treating the right sickness is an important part of getting well.

Many people are seeking to overcome addictions or spiritual strongholds by trying to cure the wrong sickness. They are medicating something that is not the problem. But if you truly want to get healthier and heal from your addictions hold on your life, you will need to address the spiritual root of the sin. You will need to address the motivation (lust, enticement, guilt, pain, and so on) that propels you toward the stronghold.

We can understand this more fully by examining God's Word and allowing His truth to lead us into a greater awareness of the root causes of addiction.

Read 2 Corinthians 10:2-5.

> *I ask that when I am present I need not be bold with the confidence with which I propose to be courageous against some, who regard us as if we walked according to the flesh. For though we walk in the flesh, we do not war according to the flesh, for the weapons of our warfare are not of the flesh, but divinely powerful for the destruction of fortresses. We are destroying speculations and every lofty thing raised up against the knowledge of God, and we are taking every thought captive to the obedience of Christ.*
> 2 CORINTHIANS 10:2-5

What does Paul mean by saying we "walk in the flesh" but "we do not war according to the flesh"?

How can we apply this principle to the spiritual strongholds we face?

Physical symptoms often have a spiritual root. While there is a time and place to treat the physical symptoms produced by a spiritual stronghold, if we never get around to treating the root cause, we will never overcome our addictions. To prevail, we need to war according to the Spirit of God working in and through us.

Describe some examples of lofty things raised up against the knowledge of God.

Share in practical terms how one takes "every thought captive" according to the will of God through Jesus Christ.

The word "lofty" can also refer to a "partition" or a divide set up in a room. Paul argued that the reason many of us remain defeated is because we fail to destroy the partition in our minds. Satan has erected a blockage in the mind which separates the knowledge of God from the thoughts of man. When the lofty partition remains in place, the truth of God does not get through in order to inform and transform the thoughts of man.

Taking every thought captive means removing the partitions and ingraining God's Word into our own thoughts. As this happens, our thoughts begin to line up with God's as opposed to the false narrative Satan continually tries to sell us. Self-help advice about being mindful may help us for a moment; true freedom from the spiritual stronghold of addiction only comes through the power of Jesus Christ.

How do we overcome the partition that separates the knowledge of God from the thoughts of man?

When God's truth no longer influences your thought patterns, you live in a state of perpetual defeat. The biblical term for this lofty partition and divided thought is "double-mindedness" (Jas. 1:8; Ps. 12:2; 119:113). It means to think in two different directions at the same time.

Consider what would happen if you tried to drive in two different directions at the same time. You would get nowhere and fast. Similarly, double-mindedness keeps you stuck, trapped, and entombed in addictive behavior and thought patterns, which prohibit you from fully reaching the destiny and purpose God has designed for you to live out.

Get out a pen or pencil and place it on the dot just below this sentence. After you do, draw in both directions simultaneously away from the dot.

I understand that I just asked you to do something that is impossible. You cannot place one pen or pencil on one dot and then draw in both directions away from the dot at the same time. It's impossible to go in two directions at once. We all realize this. But what we often forget is that it is also not possible to think about the things of God and the things of the world at the same time. You have to choose which one you will set your mind on: truth or lies. But you can't have truth and lies at the same time. Just like a little bit of arsenic will ruin an entire pot of chili, a lie will taint the truth causing it to be ineffective in its role to set you free from spiritual strongholds.

Why is it important to understand that truth and lies cannot mix and still retain the power of the truth to set a person free?

Why is mixing the truth with a lie a trap we are so prone to return to?

Can you identify ways you may have been mixing in worldly wisdom or lies with God's Word, thus tainting the Word of God and stripping it of its power in your life?

What steps can you take to focus more fully and completely on the truth of God's Word?

Pray right now and commit your mind to the Lord. Seek ways you can reduce or remove worldly and secular influence on your thinking. Let God break the bonds of addictive behavior in your life by allowing His truth to take root in your thoughts and your heart. Ask God to make you aware of anything (behavior, relationships, entertainment) that you need to reduce or remove in order to better protect and preserve your thoughts according to His truth.

REVERSING
EMOTIONAL
CONSEQUENCES

Start

Welcome to Group Session 5 of the U-Turns Bible Study.

How did last session's discussion on addiction help you think about this issue differently?

Moving on from addiction, this week we will see how to secure a u-turn from another prevalent and distressing issue.

What are some common causes of anxiety and worry in our culture today?

Why do you think as humanity has advanced technologically and materially that the rates of worry and anxiety have increased rather than decreased?

Worry plagues us, now more than ever before. So many things give people anxiety, fear, and frustration. Emotional calm and personal peace seem as elusive as the abominable snowman in the desert of Arizona. People need a u-turn to leave emotional strongholds in the past and regain a calmness of spirit.

Mental anguish can set in like a paintbrush over a person's mind applying coat after coat after coat of new layer of anxiety and fear. When too many layers have been applied, it becomes increasingly difficult to strip away. That's why it is so important to address the root of worry and anxiety. We're going to look at that in this week's session on how to reverse emotional consequences in our lives.

Invite someone to pray, then watch the video teaching.

Watch

Use these statements to follow along as you watch video session 5.

Concern, you control. Worry controls you.

The key to emotional stability is shifting your priority.

Most people are crucified between two thieves: yesterday and tomorrow.

Video sessions available at lifeway.com/UTurns or with a subscription to smallgroup.com

Discuss

Use the following questions to discuss the video teaching.

Read Isaiah 26:3 together.

You will keep him in perfect peace,
Whose mind is stayed on You,
Because he trusts in You.
ISAIAH 26:3, NKJV

Have you ever taken your eyes off the road when you are driving? At times a driver might look down at something in the car or out the window. Inevitably, when a person takes his or her eyes off of the road, it isn't long before the hands start to shift directions as well.

Where you look often determines where you drive. Similarly, where you set your mind will determine where you direct your emotions. If and when your mind focuses on Christ and the assuring Word of God, your emotions will ground themselves in the truth of His care. But in those times when you set your mind on the worries, fears, unknowns, or chaos prevalent in life, your emotions will reflect those thoughts as well. Scripture tells us in one of the most straightforward antidotes to worry and anxiety ever given: Peace results when you choose to place your thoughts on God.

Why is peace is so closely tied to what a person thinks?

How can a person gain greater control over what he or she thinks?

What are some subtle strategies Satan uses to guide someone's mind to thoughts which cultivate insecurity, anxiety, and worry?

What are some counter-tactics you could deploy to overcome Satan's strategies?

Dr. Evans makes a very important distinction in this week's video teaching when he says, "The difference between concern and worry is this: Concern you control. Worry controls you. It leads to an irritable, frustrating life. Worry removes calm and replaces it with mental and emotional chaos. Worry ruins the show of your life. Having legitimate concerns and mapping out a plan to deal with them is fine. But when your concerns own you, Jesus says, 'Don't do it.'"

Describe the difference between worry and concern.

What steps can you take to keep your legitimate concerns from drifting into unhelpful worry?

In the video Dr. Evans mentioned that the average head of hair has around 100,000 strands of hair, yet the Bible tells us that God is aware of even when a hair falls from a person's head. He went on to share how many atoms are present in a drop of water, and yet God holds the entire universe together with seemingly no effort at all. If He can take care of our vast and complicated universe, He will sustain your life.

Why do you think God chose to illustrate the solution to our stress and worry through an example like the one about our hair (Luke 12:7)?

How does worry lead us to be dismissive of God's power, strength, and loving care?

Close the session with prayer.

PRAYER

Father, You are in control, and You care deeply for Your creation. Help us to let go of my worry, fear, and anxiety by choosing to place our thoughts on the wonder of Your Word and the power of Your promises. Continue to remind us when our thoughts rise up to worry so that we can take them captive to Christ and return to a mental state of rest. In Christ's name, amen.

Securing Your U-Turn

Use the following u-turn diagram to help you process the specific u-turn you need to make based on this week's teaching. Use the questions and statements on the next page to guide you through this exercise.

Where I need to be:

_____

The change I need to make:

_____

Where I am now:

_____

QUESTIONS TO CONSIDER

*Use these questions and statements to help you
fill out the diagram on the previous page.*

**What controls your thoughts also controls your emotions. What unhealthy
thoughts do you need to reject and adjust?**

How can you challenge your unhealthy thoughts with the Word of God?

**List your common worries. Consider what the Word of God has to say
about those worries. Hint: there are hundreds of passages of Scripture
that tell us not to fear or worry—a simple Google search or a concordance
can help you locate them.**

Hit the Streets
CALMING EMOTIONS IN A CRISIS

Living a life of peace and calm starts in your thoughts. What you allow yourself to think about will have a direct impact on the level of peace you experience. This truth is why Satan seeks to influence and infiltrate people's thoughts through music, movies, social media, and so many other ways. Whoever or whatever controls the thoughts controls the emotions.

I want to give you three solid steps you can apply to set you on the path toward full emotional freedom. If you will faithfully commit yourself to these three steps, you will begin to enjoy a greater sense of peace and calm in your life.

1. CHALLENGE YOUR THOUGHTS.

Don't readily receive all thoughts in your mind as being life-producing or calm-inducing thoughts. Challenge your thoughts by holding them up against the standard of God's Word. If and when your thoughts do not align with God's promises in His Word or in obedience to His commands, you can identify those thoughts as contrary to His will for you. Allowing them to remain will lead only to greater emotional turmoil.

2. CHANGE YOUR THOUGHTS.

Once you've identified a particular thought that runs contrary to God's truth, you can make the choice to change it. A thought can be changed either by releasing it and letting it go or by seeking out more information and clarity on the subject based on God's Word. Change your thoughts so that they are in sync with the truth of God and His law of love. That will point you in the direction of peace.

3. CHARGE YOUR THOUGHTS.

Make spending time in God's Word a regular occurrence. Meditate on His Word. Read His Word for a greater understanding. As you explore God's truth and what His perspective is on a matter, it will charge your thoughts with life-giving hope. Just like a car battery needs to be charged in order for it to fulfill its function, our thoughts need to be charged with the energy of God's truth in order for them to produce the peace and calm we crave in our emotional lives.

As you go through your day, thoughts will come and go. Seek to pay greater attention to the thoughts you experience. While you increase your awareness of your thoughts, you will be in a better position to challenge them, change them when necessary, and offer them an ongoing charge of God's perspective on a matter. These three things are certain to elevate the level of peace and calm you are free to enjoy.

What thoughts do you need to take captive, release, or rethink to be obedient to God?

BIBLE STUDY 1

GOD'S PRESCRIPTION FOR PEACE

When a doctor prescribes a medication that has been designed to make you well, you are responsible for doing two things. First, you must get your prescription filled. Yet a piece of paper alone, even with your solution written on it, will accomplish nothing in bringing about the healing you desire. After you go and fill your prescription with the medicine you need, you need to do a second thing. You need to take it according to the directions.

If you fail to do either of those things, you will have reduced the prescriptions effectiveness in combating whatever illness or ailment that plagues you. Similarly, in Matthew 6:25-34, Jesus gives us a prescription for overcoming worry and obtaining optimal peace. But we will only experience peace if we fully fill our thoughts with and then apply what He says.

Read Matthew 6:25-34.

Jesus wanted us to obey this teaching, and He offered no exceptions. Why then do we riddle ourselves with worry?

What would it look like to obey this advice every day? What would change if we did?

Jesus gives us two key directions in following His prescription for peace. First, He tells us not to worry. Then, He also tells us we are to seek first the kingdom of God. The first part of our prescription for peace involves three key words: Do not worry.

Problems can arise when people fail to realize that these three words carry no weight in helping achieve personal peace unless they are applied.

Read the following verses and summarize each one in your own words. After you summarize the verse, give the one main action item Jesus is asking us to do in His prescription for peace:

> *For this reason I say to you, do not be worried about*
> *your life, as to what you will eat or what you will drink;*
> *nor for your body, as to what you will put on. Is not life*
> *more than food, and the body more than clothing?*
> MATTHEW 6:25

Summary:

Action Item:

> *Do not worry then, saying, "What will we eat?" or*
> *"What will we drink?" or "What will we wear for clothing?"*
> MATTHEW 6:31

Summary:

Action Item:

> *So do not worry about tomorrow; for tomorrow will care*
> *for itself. Each day has enough trouble of its own.*
> MATTHEW 6:34

Summary:

Action Item:

The key to emotional security involves the first step of obeying Jesus' directions not to worry. But as we explore this passage more deeply, we discover the second aspect of Jesus' prescription for peace—prioritizing God as preeminent in your life.

When we shift our thoughts onto God first, we are shifting our priorities. Remember, as a person thinks, so is he or she (Prov. 23:7 NKJV). God must take center stage in your life. He must be positioned first. What that means is that God's ways, will, and perspective must dominate all you think, do, and say. God must not be just one element or source that you go to deal with your worry. Rather, God must be the stabilizing Source you seek. Everything else must be secondary. When you put God first, His kingdom rule will usher in peace and calm in your emotions.

Read Matthew 6:33. What does it mean to "seek first His kingdom"?

What results from seeking God's kingdom and His righteousness first?

The "kingdom" is the realm of God's overarching rule. The kingdom agenda is the visible manifestation of the comprehensive rule of God over every area of life. When we read that we are to seek God's "righteousness" in Matthew 6:33, that means we are to seek His standard. Righteousness is set by God's own standard of holiness, rule, and purity. We are to aim to live up to His standard in all we do or say. Whether we accomplish that aim every time is another story. But failure to do so should never diminish our priority to live according to God's righteous standard as an aspect of daily life.

When God rules over all, and we seek to make our decisions based on what He has revealed in His Word as truth, then we will be seeking first the kingdom and His righteousness. We will be living out the principle established for us in this passage and, as a result, we will experience His provision of "all these things." That's not to say God will give us everything we want. But He will give us everything we need, and once we learn the secret of contentment (Phil. 4:11-13), we will also discover the pathway to peace.

Read Psalm 55:22.

Cast your burden upon the LORD *and He will sustain you; He will never allow the righteous to be shaken.*
PSALM 55:22

Describe what it means to "be shaken."

How can Psalm 55:22 still be true when difficulties arise and troubles ensue in a believer's life?

How would you describe the practical process of casting "your burden" on God?

Have you ever gone fishing, or seen someone fishing? When a fisherman casts a line into the lake, does he or she still hold onto the hook as well? Is it possible to cast a line with a hook and bait on the end of it while simultaneously holding onto it? No, because these two actions are mutually exclusive. To cast something means to release it far from you. Similarly, when you cast your burdens on God, that doesn't mean you are to also hold onto the burdens yourself. You need to let them go. God loves you more than you could ever know or understand. Trust Him to take your burdens and exchange them with His presence of peace as you seek Him first over all other things.

Pray about your personal priorities. Ask God to reveal to you areas in your life where He does not hold first place. Maybe it's a relationship that carries more influence on your thoughts and decisions than God and His Word. Or maybe it's a stronghold that dictates what you do. Whatever the case, ask God to make it clear to you so that you can repent and turn from that which is holding you hostage in your emotions.

BIBLE STUDY 2

THINKING IT THROUGH

Your thoughts are not always your own. They may seem like your own. They may feel like your own. But Satan has unique ways of placing thoughts in our minds in order to seek to lead us contrary to God's will. These thoughts may come through media we consume, the conversations we have, or the books and articles we read. Whatever the origin, the intention remains the same—to lead you astray from God's truth.

In fact, Satan is a master at planting thoughts in your mind and making you think they are your own. Thoughts of self-defeat, anxiety, and fear are his specialties. Some of his favorites might sound like this:

> *"I can't overcome low self-esteem and the comparison trap."*
> *"I can't be free from this emotional bondage."*
> *"I can't resist these old habits of falling into depression."*

Those are just a few. He's got many more. But in order for you to overcome the damaging effects of thoughts like these, you must stop believing the lies. They are lies. You can be free. You can overcome. You can resist destructive habits, or be lifted from depression.

Read 2 Corinthians 5:17.

> *Therefore if anyone is in Christ, he is a new creature; the old things passed away; behold, new things have come.*
> 2 CORINTHIANS 5:17.

What are some of the old things which have passed away?

Why is it important to let go of the past limitations of the flesh and abide in the newness of God's Spirit?

Christ sets people free. He starts with the acknowledgment that the new life you have in Him will enables you to overcome the lies the enemy has spoken to you. The Spirit of God in you has the power to overcome whatever it is that is holding you down. Satan's lies and his darkness will dissolve in the light of God's presence and truth.

Read Paul's words.

> *I can do all things through Him who strengthens me.*
> PHILIPPIANS 4:13

In what ways can God's "strengthening" of us help us to overcome emotional strongholds?

How can we live with the awareness of that strength?

What are some of the more difficult emotional strongholds you need help to overcome?

List three practical things you can start doing this week in order to access a greater level of God's strength:

1. _____

2. _____

3. _____

As you seek to access more and more of God's strength in order to become stronger yourself, you will quickly discover the awesome truth that you are not alone. You are valuable, treasured, and worthy of attention. God is right there for you, waiting to help you. You can overcome whatever emotional stronghold you face because you are not on your own. God longs to reveal His presence and power to you, but that will only come when you let go of what you know. Learn to rely on God and His strength instead of trying to overcome by approaches rooted in your flesh. Put your focus on what God can do, not on what you have done or what has happened to you in the past.

Have you ever taken the time to think about what you think? If not, spend a few minutes just observing your thoughts as they enter your mind. Try not to judge them as right or wrong. Just observe. What are some observations you had on your thoughts?

Consider the following Scripture.

And do not be conformed to this world, but be transformed by the renewing of your mind, so that you may prove what the will of God is, that which is good and acceptable and perfect.
ROMANS 12:2

What does it mean to "renew your mind?"

What are some practical steps you can take to "renew your mind" on a regular basis?

When a basketball player has a tough time in his game, we say he's in a "slump." This is not unusual; athletes go through slumps all of the time. But an athlete can't stay in that slump; at some point, he or she has to rebound. They have to bounce back.

Being bound by an emotional stronghold can be akin to living in a slump. You aren't able to accomplish what you know you can, enjoy the experiences like you were made to enjoy them, or even fulfill the purpose God has destined you to fulfill. You are still on the team—in God's kingdom family—but you are not living up to your potential. While it is normal and natural to fall into a slump from time to time, it is not normal or natural to remain there. You can't stay there. You must be about the business of getting out. You must seek the u-turn that will lead you out of the slump and back toward God's power.

Renewing the mind, as seen in Romans 12:2, leads to a life of purpose in the will of God. How does living with purpose affect your emotions?

Compare and contrast two seasons in your life when you felt like you knew your purpose and were living it along with another season where you did not fully know your purpose. Write your thoughts below.

What is a key principle you learned from comparing these two seasons?

Father, give me greater strength from You in order to overcome the different emotional strongholds that pop up in my heart and mind. I seek Your will through seeking a closer, abiding relationship with You and Your Word. I want to know my purpose and live it fully and completely so that I can be blessed with that which is good, acceptable, and perfect. Please help me to take control of my thoughts so that they no longer dictate to me what my emotions will be. In Christ's name, amen.

Week 6

REVERSING IRREVERSIBLE CONSEQUENCES

Start

Welcome to Group Session 6 of the U-Turns Bible Study.

What is the most essential truth you've learned from this study so far?

Rehearsing past sins and becoming aware of the effects of negative consequences in our lives is no doubt painful, so thank you for sticking with it. This week, we're going to be talking about the final u-turn for this study.

What are some common responses to ongoing negative consequences? For example: hopelessness, grief, and so forth.

In what ways can thoughts and feelings of hopelessness contribute to a person remaining stuck in a bad situation?

As you've thought about your choices over the past you weeks, you may be tempted to feel like your choices have set you on an irreversible course toward doom and gloom. You may see no way to recover from your failures. But the good news is that if you are willing to take a u-turn, God has a u-turn with your name on it.

Invite someone to pray, then watch the video teaching.

Watch

Use these statements to follow along as you watch video session 6.

God uses retests to give us a new opportunity in what
appeared to be a irreversible situation.

God can hit a bullseye with a crooked stick.

Discuss

Use the following questions to discuss the video teaching.

Read Matthew 19:26 together.

And looking at them Jesus said to them, "With people this is impossible, but with God all things are possible."
MATTHEW 19:26

Studying the nature and effects of negative consequences in our lives can be daunting. The lingering consequences of sin might produce thoughts of hopelessness or despair. Yet hopelessness and despair, if left to simmer, can keep a person stuck on the wrong road for far too long. Reversing what seems like irreversible consequences may, in fact, be impossible for people to do in their own strength. But nothing is impossible with God.

Why is it important to focus on God's power as opposed to your own when it comes to challenging and seemingly impossible situations?

What lengths did God go to in order to reverse the negative consequences in your life?

Just one mistake, or one bad decision, or one bad choice can ruin a whole life. Many of us can look back and wish we hadn't said it, done it, gone there, considered it, or took part in damaging decisions. In fact, far too many believers are still reeling from the repercussions of wrong choices, desperate for a u-turn. Maybe you're desperate for a u-turn too. Thankfully, God provides the perfect u-turn that is available to all people through the life, death, and resurrection of Jesus Christ. He who did not spare the life of His own Son has done everything necessary to secure the u-turn you need.

How do negative choices tend to compound and lead to more negative choices?

In the video, Dr. Evans asked us to consider some important questions. He said, "Do you feel like there's a curse on your life? Something you did when you were a teenager, something you did in that a relationship, something you did illegally or immorally and you feel cursed? You feel like God is nowhere to be found, and you are in excruciating pain over it. You can't forget it. It haunts you." God can set you free and use your story to help others.

When has God's reversed a situation in your life that seemed irreversible? What did you learn from that experience?

God longs for us to learn, and consequences help us learn. He allows discipline to instruct us toward a greater awareness of His kingdom values so that we might reflect Him more accurately. God will often give us many opportunities to repent and return to Him in what appeared to be an irreversible situation. By putting us in the same situation we were in when we failed previously, He leads us to deeper discoveries.

How does the discipline of God allow us to experience His grace?

Hopelessness anchors the soul to negative consequences like nothing else. If you believe there is no way God could ever turn your situation around, then you have already determined the outcome. God may be (and probably is) willing to give you a retest to set you on the right path. But you must believe in His grace and mercy in order to receive it.

PRAYER

Father, You have the power to turn anything around in our lives. You can restore what the locusts have stolen (Joel 2:25). We do not want to stand in the way of what You are doing in our lives to turn things around. Help us to be humble enough to repent but also confident enough in You and Your love to recognize Your hand of mercy and grace. Help us not to miss the u-turn you've provided. Thank You for leading us there. In Christ's name, amen.

Securing Your U-Turn

Use the following u-turn diagram to help you process the specific u-turn you need to make based on this week's teaching. Use the questions and statements on the next page to guide you through this exercise.

Where I need to be:

_____

The change I need to make:

_____

Where I am now:

_____

QUESTIONS TO CONSIDER

Use these questions and statements to help you
fill out the diagram on the previous page.

Are there sins in your past that you feel God would not forgive you for? Read Hebrews 8:12. Why is this way of thinking a lie from the devil?

If God is willing to forgive any sin, why are you unwilling to take all your sins to Him?

How can you remember daily the depth of grace that God has given you in Jesus Christ? How might remembering this change the way you think about your failures and short comings?

Hit the Streets
RETAKING OUR THOUGHTS

One of the most important passages of Scripture for each of us to memorize and come to understand the truth within it is found in Isaiah 55:8-9. This chapter speaks to the importance of returning to God so that He will have compassion on you. It urges us to seek the Lord and find Him. To call on Him and know that He is near. It asks us to embrace the u-turn God has for us. But, perhaps even more important than all of that, this chapter reminds us who we are and who God is. We are finite. God is infinite. We see through a mirror dimly. God sees past, present, and future simultaneously. We comprehend little. God comprehends all. We think we know the way. God really knows the way.

> *"For My thoughts are not your thoughts,*
> *nor are your ways My ways," declares the LORD.*
> *"For as the heavens are higher than the earth,*
> *so are My ways higher than your ways*
> *and My thoughts than your thoughts."*
> ISAIAH 55:8-9

We can learn two key principles from this powerful passage.

1. GOD'S THOUGHTS ARE NOT OUR THOUGHTS.

They are higher. Once we realize that God sees so much more than us, we can let go of trying to manipulate things according to our own understanding. God is intimately involved with the minute details of His creation, yet He also stands above all creation. He sees all. He knows all. He comprehends all. Thus, He can consider all. We are finite and can only consider what we have come across at some point in time. In order to experience a reversal of seemingly irreversible circumstances in our lives, we must trust, follow, and obey the One who knows and understands all. We must look to Him and His Word as our ultimate guidance.

2. GOD'S WAYS ARE NOT OUR WAYS.

They are higher. Just as God's thoughts are beyond ours, His ways are also much more sophisticated than any plan or path we could concoct. God knows all the options on the table, and then some, so we would be wise to let Him lead. If God can guide an entire nation across a sea to escape an oncoming army, He can do anything. He is not bound by time or matter like we are. Look to God to show you your next step in order to reverse the seemingly irreversible scenario you may be facing right now.

In what areas are you relying on your own thoughts and your own ways when you need to rely on God's thoughts and God's ways?

BIBLE STUDY 1

GOD'S SOLUTIONS SOMETIMES LOOK SLIGHTLY ... OFF

God sees all. God knows all. God understands all. Because of this, His ways and His thoughts are not on the same level as us. His direction or guidance in our lives may sound strange. We may question why He allows or allowed what He did. We may scratch our head and try to figure out His plan. But, in the end, Isaiah 55:8-9 reminds us that we may never figure out God's plan on this side of heaven. His thoughts are not our thoughts, and His ways are not our ways.

His perspective is simply so much higher, broader, wiser, grander, and transcendent than ours. That's why faith is critical in a believer's life. Faith demonstrates, through our actions, that we trust God even when we don't understand Him.

Why is it difficult to trust God when you do not understand what He's doing?

How has God proven Himself faithful to you when you followed Him despite not understanding what He was asking you to do?

What does it look like to trust God's heart when you do not understand His hand?

To trust God's heart means you choose to trust that He has your best interest in mind when He guides you. Trusting God's heart gives you the freedom to move forward according to His leading in your life, even when where He's leading you doesn't make sense. If you truly believe that God loves you and wants what is best for you, you do not need to understand the path He is taking you on to trust that the destination is good.

Read Romans 8:28.

And we know that God causes all things to work together for good to those who love God, to those who are called according to His purpose.
ROMANS 8:28

What comfort does this verse provide in the middle of confusion?

How have you experienced the truth of this verse with u-turns God has given you in the past?

Obedience that requires faith delights the heart of God. You can say you trust God, but if your actions don't align with the truth of those words, then they are just words. Actions speak louder than words. God will often allow us to experience what seems like an irreversible situation to remind us of the substance of our faith in Him. This is how all things work together for good, even things that seem far from good.

What does it mean to have active faith in practice?

In what ways does your faith show trust in God's character and His Word?

Read 2 Kings 5:1-14 from this week's video teaching.

There are times in our lives, as we see in the biblical example of Naaman in 2 Kings 5 when we lack faith. Naaman did not want to go to the Jordan and dip seven times as the prophet had instructed him. He thought that solution was stupid, and he didn't want to look like a fool. Fortunately for him, Naaman had others around him who would encourage him to demonstrate active faith in the words of the prophet, no matter how foolish it made him feel.

Great leaders, and great people, listen to others who may know more than they know. It's okay to lean on someone else's faith when yours is waning. I call that "piggy-backing" on someone else's faith. This is important because sometimes others see more clearly than you do because your vision has become blurred by the pain of your present reality. Greatness doesn't always mean knowing the right way to go. Often it means letting those who know the right way to guide you. Greatness comes wrapped in humility, or it isn't greatness at all.

When have you learned from someone who saw a situation clearer than you?

How do we cultivate the humility to seek and receive counsel from others?

What kind of humility is required of us to follow God's ways?

When you are willing to let go of your own way, you become freed up to follow God's way. You have to release your own plans to experience the power and God's restoration in your life. No matter how much money, notoriety, or esteem a person may have on this planet, it's God alone who makes miracles. And sometimes, God seeks to remind us this by allowing us to be in situations that no man can fix. He allows our mess to get so bad that man-made solutions no longer exist. He does this so He can demonstrate He alone is God.

Read Proverbs 14:12.

There is a way which seems right to a man,
but its end is the way of death.
PROVERBS 14:12

How does the wisdom of this verse address our human need for personal control?

What are some ways we can align our plans under God's rule?

God's solutions aren't always difficult. They are often so simple that we brush them off in our human wisdom—similar to how Naaman did in the biblical account we studied in this week's lesson.

It's easy to think, "Surely it's not that easy," as we go and try something more complex of our own to fix whatever mess we face. But God's solutions and His miracles throughout Scripture often defined themselves as a simple act of faith. A restored spirit through repentance. Holding up a rod. Putting feet in water. Marching around an enormous wall seven times. Or, even dipping in the muddy Jordan River.

Pray and ask God to reveal to you or remind you of a path or action step He is asking you to carry out in order to experience true restoration and healing in your life. Ask Him to clarify it for you and to give you the courage to follow Him. If you do not already have a group of committed kingdom disciples in your life, seek God's direction to lead you to those individuals who will encourage you to follow Him in faith in all you do.

BIBLE STUDY 2

THE SOLUTION IS OFTEN SIMPLE

One of the most common mistakes we make when we are seeking God's solutions instead of our own is to assume that God's solutions are more complicated than our own. We figure since He sits above all and outside of all, His solutions must be beyond our comprehension in complexity as well. But that isn't always the case.

Read the following biblical examples of God providing a solution and write out what the main solution was in each case.

> *When they came to Capernaum, those who collected the two-drachma tax came to Peter and said, "Does your teacher not pay the two-drachma tax?" He said, "Yes." And when he came into the house, Jesus spoke to him first, saying, "What do you think, Simon? From whom do the kings of the earth collect customs or poll-tax, from their sons or from strangers?" When Peter said, "From strangers," Jesus said to him, "Then the sons are exempt. However, so that we do not offend them, go to the sea and throw in a hook, and take the first fish that comes up; and when you open its mouth, you will find a shekel. Take that and give it to them for you and Me."*
> MATTHEW 17:24-27

Problem:

Solution:

> *As He passed by, He saw a man blind from birth ... "We must work the works of Him who sent Me as long as it is day; night is coming when no one can work. While I am in the world, I am the Light of the world." When He had said this, He spat on the ground, and made clay of the spittle, and applied the clay to his eyes, and said to him, "Go, wash in the pool of Siloam" (which is translated, Sent). So he went away and washed, and came back seeing."*
> JOHN 9:1,4-7

Problem:

Solution:

> *Now Naaman, captain of the army of the king of Aram, was a great man with his master, and highly respected, because by him the* LORD *had given victory to Aram. The man was also a valiant warrior, but he was a leper … Elisha sent a messenger to him, saying, "Go and wash in the Jordan seven times, and your flesh will be restored to you and you will be clean." … So he went down and dipped himself seven times in the Jordan, according to the word of the man of God; and his flesh was restored like the flesh of a little child and he was clean."*
>
> 2 KINGS 5:1,10

Problem:

Solution:

Isaiah 55:8 didn't say that God's thoughts involve more complex and difficult solutions. It said that God's thoughts are different than ours. Far too often we miss the u-turn in our lives because we try to complicate things with our own solutions. We try to get our hands in the mix when God has it already planned out. We increase our pain and extend our misery because we refuse to let go and trust that He knows best. All the while God stands waiting, thinking—if only you would just dip. It ain't that deep. Just do as I say, and you are clean.

Never let your pride keep you from solving your problem. Do what God says. You will discover, as Naaman did, that God knows what He is doing.

Record an experience where God's solution seemed too simple to you, so you chose to ignore it. If this has never happened to you, can you recall a biblical example where this happened? What were the results?

Why do we often feel that overcomplicated or complex solutions have a better opportunity for success than simple, straightforward ones?

God's plan for your u-turn may not make sense. It may seem too simple. Similarly, you may not see the outcome you desire right at the start. But it's important to remember that a partial u-turn is no u-turn at all.

You have to complete the u-turn to get back on the road and headed in the other direction. What happens to a driver, and the vehicle, who only does a partial u-turn?

Partial u-turns will just take you off-roading, where things will get even bumpier and potentially disastrous. If Naaman had decided to stop dipping after the first few times because he felt dumb or didn't see any results, he wouldn't have been healed. Naaman dipped seven times. His healing didn't come in partial increments. He was healed after he fully obeyed what the prophet said to do.

Whatever God asks you to do, do it fully even if you don't see immediate results. Even if your faith falters more than it grows. Even if you doubt the process. Obey fully. Do it because God's ways are not your ways, and His thoughts are not your thoughts. Do it because you put your trust in Him by faith.

What is God asking you to do fully that you are only doing partially? How is that working out for you?

At the end of this study, what u-turns do you feel God is leading you to embrace?

How has your faith grown through this study?

Whatever you believe God is asking you to do, as long as you have tested it to see that it aligns with His revealed will in His Word, do all of it. He can turn your life around and set you on the path to living out the fullness of your destiny. But this will only happen if you yield to Him through a personal surrender of your ways, thoughts, and goals. Let God guide you according to the pathway He knows is best for you in this season of your life. Trust Him to work out the details. He is the great God of redemption and restoration, and He has a great plan just for you.

Let's close our time together in this Bible study with prayer. Heavenly Father, thank You for the blessing of second, third, and fourth chances. Thank You that You enable me to take a u-turn when I wind up going the wrong way in life. Show me where I need to turn around, Lord. Get me on the right path. Help me to also help others who may need a u-turn in their lives. Thank You for answering these requests. In Christ's name, amen.

D-GROUP GUIDE

If you're reading this, you likely care about discipleship. You desire to be a kingdom disciple living under God's kingdom agenda. Being in a small group or a Sunday School class is one means believers use to go deeper in the Christian life. However, increasingly, people want a closer and more tight-knit community. To this end, we've provided a guide to facilitate those kinds of small groups. What is a D-group? As opposed to an open small group or a Sunday School class (meaning everyone is welcome), a D-Group is a closed group that three or four people join by invitation and commitment.

What's the purpose of a D-Group?

These groups are for Christians who desire to walk more closely with the Lord. The smaller nature of the group allows a more concentrated level of accountability and opens up discussions that are more personal than in a standard group meeting.

Why do I need a D-group?

We're not meant to live the Christian life alone. You'll need support as you seek to live as a kingdom disciple. Opening yourself up to people in a smaller environment encourages participation from you and from those who may not feel comfortable opening up in a larger group.

Additionally, D-Groups give others permission to speak into your life for encouragement, accountability, and prayer.

What's required of me?

The goal of these groups is deeper discipleship and accountability. Achieving this goal requires commitment. Plan to meet for one hour. Be willing to attend and participate each week. Be willing to be open and honest about your spiritual condition and about ways you're struggling. Be willing to hold what's said in the group in confidence. What's said should remain in the group as a means of building trust with one another. Finally, be willing to pray and support one another. Allow the relationships to extend beyond the group meeting itself.

How to Use These Guides

A D-Group guide is provided for each week of this study. These guides are meant to be used in addition to the weekly group session but can be also used by people who aren't meeting with a group. However, these guides work best if participants have seen the week's video teaching by Dr. Evans. Each D-Group guide is one short page and includes the following elements:

Summary

A summary of the week's main point and big ideas. These are meant to give you a quick reference point.

D-Group questions

These open-ended questions are designed to encourage each other to open up about their struggles and successes for the purposes of growth and accountability.

Weekly challenge

A simple exercise to complete over the next week and report back to the group. These challenges are meant to take the truth of the session and apply it to your life and relationships.

U-Turns

Free to Choose Your Direction.

God has given us a choice. Each of us has been given the ability to choose life or death in everything we think, do, or say. Each moment is an opportunity to move forward into favor or backward into consequences and adversity. God doesn't make these choices for us. We have been blessed with free will to choose the course of our lives. The life we live today exists as the compounded result of a myriad choices we've freely made along the way. When we choose the path of life, we receive blessings. When we choose the path of death, we suffer the consequences of our sin.

The power of a u-turn is the power to realize that you are free to choose your destination. No matter how far you have driven from God, He will always supply a u-turn to those looking to turn around.

> **Read Deuteronomy 30:15-20 together.**
>
> **Are you a person who likes to follow the outlined path or choose your own way? How does that tendency show up in your relationship with God?**
>
> **Share a time when you have chosen the path of life and another when you've chosen the path of death. What did you learn from each experience?**
>
> **Why is it important to understand that choices have consequences that we cannot control? How would your decision-making process change if you were more aware of this truth?**

WEEKLY CHALLENGE

As you go through the week, pause a couple of times to evaluate your choices. Which ones are bringing life? Which ones are bringing consequences? Text or email your D-group and share one thing you're learning.

U-Turns

The Key to Your Reversal

Read Ezekiel 18:25 together.

Ezekiel teaches that repentance includes both turning from wickedness and practicing righteousness. Repentance is the master key to unlocking the kind of blessing and life we all desire to find.

Biblical repentance is "the internal decision and determination to turn from sin." While forgiveness is entirely based on the sinless sacrifice of Jesus Christ, repentance still involves a determination to turn from sin. The goal of repentance is the restoration of fellowship with God. Our u-turns are dependent upon our willingness to repent of our sins and pursue the Lord.

Share about the first time you felt led to repent of your sins and to turn to Jesus for forgiveness.

We often think of repentance as being the entry point of the Christian faith. Why should repentance characterize all of our lives as believers?

How does unconfessed sin hinder your relationship with God? How does it hinder your relationship with other people?

Are there any steps you need to take this week to repair a broken relationship—either with God or another person? If so, what?

WEEKLY CHALLENGE

If you identified an area of repentance above, pursue reconciliation with the one you have wronged and share with at least one member of this D-group what that experience was like.

U-Turns

Reversing Idolatrous Consequences

Read 2 Chronicles 33:1-20 together.

Manasseh was raised in a faithful home. His father was Hezekiah, a righteous king. But, even so, he chose to do evil. He promoted and led a culture of evildoers and idolaters. Manasseh built high places where false gods could be praised and worshiped. He led his own family astray, sacrificing his own children to these idols. What's more, he led his whole nation astray. The entire nation wound up worshiping idols because their leader took them in that direction.

Because of that, judgment fell. God had to break Manasseh of his personal pride. God humbled him. God let things get really bad so that they could ultimately get a lot better. Loss revealed his idol and empowered his u-turn.

Dr. Evans defined an idol as any person, place, thing, or idea that becomes your source. What are those things in your life that tend to draw you away from God? Is it a job, hobby, relationship, or something else?

Why is it helpful for us to be aware of our idols?

Why is it good to share our struggles with other people? Have you ever done this? If so, what did you learn from it?

What specific steps can you take this week to make a u-turn from pride or idolatry? Even if it is a small step, take that step.

WEEKLY CHALLENGE

Spend concentrated time in prayer, asking God to reveal your hidden idols. Think about a few practical steps you can take this week to make a u-turn from pride and idolatry. Even if it is a small step, take that step. For the sake of accountability, share the steps you're taking with others in this D-group. Check in with one another and continue to pray.

U-Turns

Reversing Addiction Consequences

Read John 8:36 together.

Addiction robs us of our freedom.

A person can be free but not really free at all. A person can live in a nation of freedoms but still be bound by emotional, relational or physical strongholds. Personal freedom sits at the root of addictions. You can't be both free and addicted at the same time. You will either be one or the other.

Fundamentally, addiction is a spiritual stronghold of negative patterns of behavior from which you cannot be released so that you can move forward in spiritual victory. We need Jesus to find the u-turns from our addictive behavior.

What are you addicted to? Attention? Binging TV shows? Achievement? How do these addictions rob you of freedom?

If you're able to identify an area of addictive behavior, what would be a better use of your time and emotional energy? How might focusing on that help you overcome your addictions?

Why is it necessary to recognize and talk about the patterns of behavior that rob us of our freedom?

WEEKLY CHALLENGE

Is there an area in your life where you need accountability in order to cultivate better habits? Who can you share your struggles with to find support?

U-Turns

Reversing Emotional Consequences

Read Isaiah 26:2.

Worry plagues us, now more than ever before. So many things give people anxiety, fear, and frustration. Emotional calm and personal peace seems as elusive as the abominable snowman in the desert of Arizona. People need a u-turn to leave emotional strongholds in the past and regain a calmness of spirit.

Where you set your mind will determine where you direct your emotions. If, and when, your mind focuses on Christ and the assuring Word of God, your emotions will ground themselves in the truth of His care. But in those times when you set your mind on the worries, fears, unknowns, or chaos prevalent in life, your emotions will reflect those thoughts as well. Scripture tells us in one of the most straightforward antidotes to worry and anxiety ever given: Peace results when you choose to place your thoughts on God.

Describe what the difference is between worry and concern. What leads you to worry?

What are some strategies you can use to deal with your fears and worries? How can your emotional troubles lead you to pursue God instead of run away from Him?

Emotional strongholds are very common problems today. How can we be people who help others apply the peace of God to their emotional turmoil?

WEEKLY CHALLENGE

Think about a friend you know who struggles with worry and anxiety. Consider what truths you might speak to him or her based on what you have learned in this week's session.

U-Turns

Reversing Irreversible Consequences

Read Matthew 19:26 and 2 Kings 5:1-14.

Studying the nature and effects of negative consequences in our lives can be daunting. The lingering consequences of sin might produce thoughts of hopelessness or despair. Yet hopelessness and despair, if left to simmer, can keep a person stuck on the wrong road for far too long. Reversing what seems like irreversible consequences may in fact be impossible for people to do in their own strength. But nothing is impossible with God.

Just one mistake, one bad decision, or one bad choice can ruin a whole life. Many of us can look back and wish we hadn't said it, done it, gone there, considered it, or took part in damaging decisions. In fact, far too many believers are still reeling from the repercussions of wrong choices, and are desperate for a u-turn. Maybe you're desperate for a u-turn too. Thankfully, God provides the perfect u-turn available to all people through the life, death, and resurrection of Jesus Christ. He who did not spare the life of His own Son has done everything necessary to secure the u-turn you need.

> **What lengths did God go to in order to reverse the negative consequences in your life? Why should we reflect upon what God has done often?**
>
> **Are there any sins or circumstances in your life for which you feel like God cannot or will not forgive you? Why should we reject this type of thinking?**
>
> **What u-turns has God given as you've worked through this study?**

WEEKLY CHALLENGE

Take time to reflect on this study. Write down three key truths you've learned and share them with at least one other person.

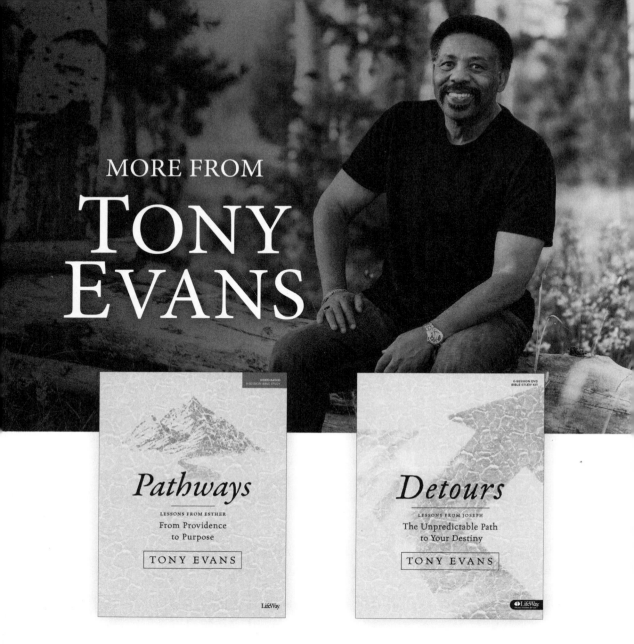

MORE FROM
TONY EVANS

PATHWAYS
From Providence to Purpose

Use the biblical account of Esther to discover your own pathway to purpose as you learn and apply principles of God's providence. (6 sessions)

Bible Study Kit $99.99
Bible Study Book $13.99

DETOURS
The Unpredictable Path to Your Destiny

Find hope in understanding that the sudden or seemingly endless detours in life are God's way of moving you from where you are to where He wants you to be. (6 sessions)

Bible Study Kit $99.99
Bible Study Book $13.99